RIVER OF BEARS

TEXT BY TOM WALKER
PHOTOGRAPHS BY LARRY AUMILLER
FOREWORD BY JOHN J. CRAIGHEAD

VOYAGEUR PRESS

River of Bears is published in cooperation with the Alaska Department of Fish and Game. Partial proceeds from the sale of this book will benefit the McNeil River Fund of the Alaska Watchable Wildlife Conservation Trust. The Wildlife Conservation Trust was created by the Alaska Conservation Foundation, in cooperation with the Alaska Department of Fish and Game, for wildlife enthusiasts to support enhanced viewing opportunities, research, and wildlife education. The Wildlife Trust is one of dozens of funds managed by the Alaska Conservation Foundation to protect the wildlife, wild lands, and wild waters of Alaska for future generations. For more information about the Alaska Conservation Foundation or to make a donation to the management of McNeil River State Game Sanctuary, please write to 430 West 7th Avenue, Suite 215, Anchorage, AK, 99501 or call 907-276-1917.

▲ ▲ ▲

Edited by Elizabeth Knight
Book design by Lou Gordon

Printed in Hong Kong
93 94 95 96 97 5 4 3 2 1

Library of Congress Cataloging-in-Publication Data

Walker, Tom, 1945–
River of bears / text by Tom Walker ; photographs by Larry Aumiller.
p. cm.
ISBN 0-89658-178-0
1. Kodiak bear—Alaska—McNeil River State Game Sanctuary. 2. McNeil River State Game Sanctuary (Alaska)
I. Aumiller, Larry, 1944– . II. Title.
QL737.C27W35 1993   92-35354
639.9'7974446—dc20   CIP

Published by
VOYAGEUR PRESS, INC.
P.O. Box 338, 123 North Second Street, Stillwater, MN 55082 U.S.A.
From Minnesota and Canada 612-430-2210; toll-free 800-888-9653

Voyageur Press books are also available at discounts for quantities for educational, fundraising, premium, or sales-promotion use. For details contact the marketing department. Please write or call for our free catalog of natural history publications.

Page 1: *A natural barrier slows and halts the upstream migration of spawning salmon, providing a feast for generations of bears.*
Pages 2–3: *A small group of bears shares the fishing sites along lower McNeil Falls. As summer progresses, brown bears become more tolerant of one another.*

CONTENTS

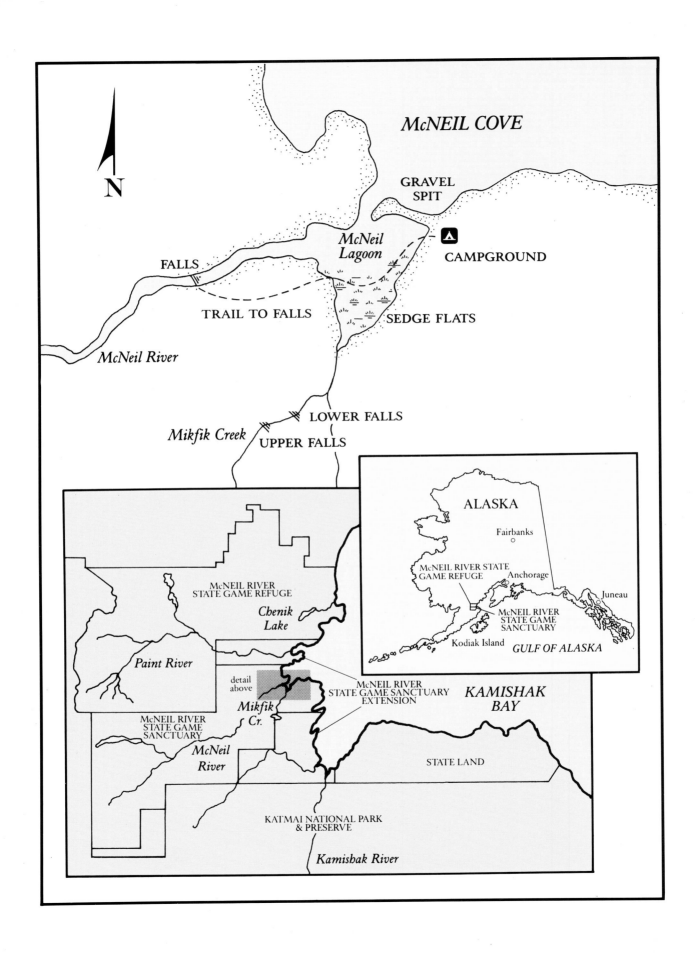

McNEIL COVE

GRAVEL SPIT

CAMPGROUND

McNeil Lagoon

FALLS

TRAIL TO FALLS

SEDGE FLATS

N

McNeil River

LOWER FALLS

Mikfik Creek   UPPER FALLS

McNEIL RIVER
STATE GAME REFUGE

Chenik Lake

Paint River

detail above

McNEIL RIVER
STATE GAME SANCTUARY
EXTENSION

KAMISHAK BAY

Mikfik Cr.

McNEIL RIVER
STATE GAME
SANCTUARY

McNeil River

STATE LAND

KATMAI NATIONAL PARK
& PRESERVE

Kamishak River

ALASKA

Fairbanks

McNEIL RIVER STATE
GAME REFUGE   Anchorage

Juneau

McNEIL RIVER
STATE GAME
SANCTUARY

Kodiak Island   *GULF OF ALASKA*

For the bears . . . and for those people who care about them

ACKNOWLEDGMENTS

ALASKA DEPARTMENT OF FISH AND GAME EMPLOYEES WES Bucher, Jim Faro, John Hyde, Colleen Matt, Rick Sinnott, Dick Sellers, Derek Stonorov, and John Trent read and commented upon draft manuscripts. Annual reports and field notes from McNeil River State Game Sanctuary provided invaluable information in the preparation of this book. Additional support material was gleaned from the professional reports and papers of Tom Bledsoe, Jim Faro, Lee Glenn, Stephen Herrero, Pauline Hessing, Colleen Matt, Sterling Miller, Harry Reynolds, Dick Sellers, John Schoen, Roger Smith, Derek Stonorov, and Larry Van Daele. Any misinterpretation of these scientific studies is solely the author's responsibility. Larry Aumiller provided technical editing and support throughout the writing process. This book would not have been possible without him.

Opposite: McNeil River State Game Sanctuary is located near the top of the Alaska Peninsula. It is 250 air miles southwest of Anchorage, Alaska's largest city, and 100 air miles west of Homer. The sanctuary campground is about two miles from either the falls of McNeil River or those of Mikfik Creek.

FOREWORD

FROM EARLIEST TIMES, BEARS HAVE CAPTURED MAN'S AWE and respect. As large, aggressive, intelligent animals, they have inspired fear, worship, and envy. But only during the last three decades have we begun to understand them. Our fear has dominated our respect, and bears have been poisoned, shot, and trapped as vermin so that in many parts of the world they are threatened or endangered. The first step in protection is understanding—a science-based knowledge of how bears and man can coexist, for coexist we must. Grizzlies and Alaskan brown bears are closely related, separated only by fine taxonomic differences distinguishing the former as *Ursus arctos horribilis* and the latter as *Ursus arctos middendorffi*. The text and photographs in this book are striking testimony to how much we have learned about the biology of the grizzly/brown bear and how well we have applied that knowledge.

A mere thirty years ago, biologists as well as laymen thought of the grizzly/brown bears as "loners." Recent studies show that they are social animals, interacting in extremely complex ways when they aggregate to feed or breed. A social hierarchy, which may number in excess of one hundred bears, is established and is generally dominated by a single alpha male. This social structure allows many aggressive animals to convene and feed in relative harmony and, thereby, conveys numerous biological advantages to the species. What the visitor sees at McNeil Falls is a phenomenon unique in the animal world, but as the saying goes, "only the tip of the iceberg is in view."

As the bears emerge from their winter dens, they gradually converge on McNeil Falls and its temporarily obstructed salmon run. They have accomplished most of their mating before arriving and are hungry following six months of winter sleep. Tradition guides them to the river and to the falls with its large, dependable supply of migrating salmon. As they arrive, the more dominant bears immediately lay claim to the choice fishing spots. These sites and others are contested as the aggregation enlarges, but eventually the most aggressive animals prevail, and a hierarchy is established—a social order in which every animal in the large aggregation recognizes every other animal, knows his or her place within the hierarchy, and behaves accordingly.

This hierarchy is reordered each year through aggressive actions that range from fierce battles to growls, a threatening stance, or a barely detectable movement of the mouth, ears, or eyes. From these and similar behavioral signals evolves an understanding where each bear recognizes its status among those assembled. This reduces aggression and minimizes the potential for physical trauma in an extremely aggressive species. It permits the population to more fully exploit a large, stable food supply, which, in turn, prepares the bear to enter a half-year period of winter sleep during which it metabolizes body fat laid down during the summer and fall. This fat is crucial to carrying the animal through the winter months until it can emerge from its den and travel to McNeil Falls to begin the cycle all over again. This is especially true of adult females that have whelped and suckled young in their dens and emerge thin, hungry, and in urgent need of protein-rich food. On arriving at the falls, an aggressive mother becomes even more assertive and will defend her fishing site, fending off some of the large males to assuage her hunger and provide for her cubs.

As the gathering of bears becomes larger, the continual interaction of bear with bear literally becomes a "ten-ring circus," where so much activity, both subtle and overt, is going on, day after day, that not even a determined bear biologist can hope to follow all the action. Only years of observations, quantitatively recorded, at McNeil and elsewhere, have allowed scientists to interpret the bears' complex behavior—to see below the tip of the iceberg.

At McNeil Falls, this unique behavioral phenomenon has been matched by a unique management phenomenon: an agency-devised program that has protected the bears while permitting safe, close-range viewing and photographing. Those who peruse this book, like those fortunate few who have visited the "river of bears," can be thankful for a vision and a wisdom seldom encountered in the management of natural resources. The uniqueness of the area and its bears was recognized in the mid-1950s and given partial protection. In 1959, the Alaska Fish and Game Department took control of the refuge, supervising guided and unguided viewing and photographic tours. In 1967, the area was established as the McNeil River State Game Sanctuary, only eight years after Alaska gained statehood. A permit system limiting visitation was established in 1973, and in 1976 Larry Aumiller was put in charge of the viewing project. His sensitive and intelligent development of the program has set a worldwide standard for wildlife viewing.

This unmatched wildlife spectacle is beautifully and ably presented in photos and text by Larry Aumiller and Tom Walker in *River of Bears*. But what you see in this book and first hand at McNeil River cannot be taken for granted. There are pending threats both to the aggregation of bears and to their habitat. The price of preserving, in perpetuity, pristine areas such as the "river of bears" is one of constant vigilance—a struggle that needs the support of all.

—John J. Craighead, Ph.D.
Chairman, Craighead Wildlife-Wildlands Institute

Overleaf: One of the greatest values of the McNeil River sanctuary is the dramatic way in which it demonstrates that bears and people can share the same space peacefully. For bears to have a future in the ever-changing world, this message—that bears are not demonic threats to human life—needs wide circulation and acceptance.

RIVER OF BEARS

Foggy tendrils, damp and chill, float across the mudflats of the cove. The tide is ebbing this early July day, exposing the sedge flats below the fifty-foot-tall conglomerate bluffs that flank the river mouth. The early morning cries of gulls and eagles are muted by the heavy wind ruffling the grass and alders. Muffled too, are footfalls of beasts large and small.

At dawn, the songs of golden-crowned sparrows and yellow warblers greet the light, while tree swallows wheel and twist above the marshes and ponds as they catch insects for their hungry broods. A line of bear tracks meanders west across the tideflats toward the mouth of the river. Somewhere a red fox barks and a raven gives its benediction to the day.

Alaska's McNeil River flows into Kamishak Bay at the head of a tiny cove protected by a long, wave-washed gravel spit. Eagles and ravens perch on the driftwood thrown upon it; shorebirds and brant feed in the lagoon in its lee. On this early July morning, an almost palpable excitement swarms in the air—the long spring wait is over, summer's bounty is at hand.

In the night, with a roaring onshore wind driving fierce waves against the bluffs, schools of salmon ran thick and fast at flood tide into the mouth of the river and made their way upstream. This morning, the river mouth is plugged with calico-patterned chum salmon.

Later, after the end of the chum salmon run, small numbers of silver salmon will add their eggs to the river's spawning gravels. Mixed in with the chums now are a very few king salmon and stray pink salmon. Even as the mature chums are struggling upstream to spawn, tiny salmon fry, hatched after a winter's incubation in the icy river water, are moving slowly downstream toward the sea. Those that survive the onslaught of wheeling gulls, terns, char, and other predators will return in four to six years from the north Pacific Ocean to spawn in these very same natal waters.

Of all the rivers that empty into Kamishak Bay, only two others support a substantial natural run of salmon.

Left: Brown bears sometimes stand on their hind legs in order to best employ their senses of sight and smell. This large male views a group of visitors that it encountered when coming over a rise near Mikfik Creek. **Inset:** *Bears search for salmon on the McNeil Cove tidal flats made green by algae growth encouraged by the light of the long summer days.*

Above: *A family of bears and a lone wolf avoid one another while searching for chum salmon on the tidal flats of McNeil Cove.* **Left:** *Thirty miles offshore, Augustine Volcano wears a dawn tiara, while beneath it McNeil Cove stirs under the wind of this early July morning.*

Upstream movement into the rest is blocked by barriers like shoals or falls cut through the upthrust, exposed bedrock. A small stream, Mikfik Creek, supports an early run of sockeye salmon. This run is an important early summer food source for bears, often available before the first grasses and other emerging plants, like wild celery, are available for forage.

This morning, there is movement at the mouth of McNeil River. A young, male wolf is trotting along the strand, chasing gulls from a few fish scraps. Pickings have been lean, and the wolf is hungry. During the night, he foraged through the driftwood berms and found and ate the contents of two semi-palmated plover nests. It barely eased the clawing talons of hunger. Although quick and agile, the wolf cannot catch a live salmon here in this deep water. He is looking for scraps and finding little. In days, however, there will be a bountiful supply, enough to feed the wolf, dozens of bears, and numerous clamorous birds.

In this swift water, even a bear would find it difficult to catch a fresh, powerful chum salmon. But upstream a short distance, a shelf of granitic cobble and boulder conglomerate creates McNeil Falls, an impediment, but not a complete barrier, to the passage of fish. Often salmon fill the deep, quiet pools below the falls, as one after another takes its turn in attempting to fight up and over the shallow rapids or through the plunging cascades. In the riffles the salmon are barely covered by water as they struggle ahead; in the chutes they launch themselves into the air as they attempt to overcome the surging white water. More often than not they are hurled back into the pools below. The urge to move upstream is powerful. Again and again they strive to cross the barrier, and in their continuing struggle they are vulnerable to predators.

On this early morning, two male bears stand by the edge of the falls and peer into the water.

One bear has taken a position near the roaring chute on the north side of the river. In midstream, fifty yards away, the other bear stands on a large rock near a swift but shallow riffle. They are aware of one another, but except for a quick look when one or the other jumps to catch a fish, they seem uninterested.

A salmon attempts to leap the roaring chute; the force of the water throws it back. With a speed belying its bulk, the waiting bear leaps and with its paws pins the fish to the rocks in the slack water next to the flume. He seizes the fish in his massive jaws and carries it up onto the rocks where he pins it again before tearing it apart. The flurry of action momentarily distracts the bear standing in midstream, and it stops to watch. But not for long. A salmon splashing in the riffle almost beneath his feet draws his attention. A lightning lunge captures it.

Over the next hour, the two bears each kill and eat eight salmon. A few fish manage to wriggle free and wash away on the current. Those that are uninjured or only slightly impaired will not be easily deterred; they will challenge the falls again. Others will die and wash downstream to the birds, smaller bears, or even perhaps to the wolf.

The bears are hungry. These are their first fish of the year and they eat almost the entirety of their catch. Later, they will be more choosy and ingest only the most nutritious parts—brains, eggs, and skin—before discarding the rest. Now the fish disappear in a few bites.

At midday another large male, bigger still than the two already on the river, appears on the bluff to the north. He emerges from one of dozens of bear trails that lace the tall grass and stands for a long time looking down at the river and sniffing the errant breezes. Finally, he lumbers off the bluff and heads directly toward the nearest bear.

The two fishing bears are always alert. They regularly scan the sloping riverbank for other bears. Their alertness pays off. The bear fishing on the bank sees the bigger bear when he is still some distance away. With head down and mouth agape, he moves away from his fishing spot in an exaggerated slow pace. The encroaching bear merely looks at the smaller bear before claiming the vacated fishing spot and assuming almost the same fishing stance as the displaced bear. In less than a minute, the newcomer has caught a fish and has carried it up onto the rocks to eat it. Downstream, the displaced bear has stopped at the edge of the river and is once again looking into the water for salmon. Its attention is occasionally distracted by the bigger bear. Several minutes later, in the same length of time it takes the newcomer to catch and eat two fish, the displaced bear catches its first salmon from the new vantage point.

The big male's short summer hair does not hide its many scars and wounds, reminders of numerous mating battles or fights over food or struggles for dominance.

In their attempts to pass over McNeil River Falls, chum salmon, which may weigh up to fourteen pounds, become easy prey for the massed brown bears.

Reggie and her maturing cub wait for chum salmon at McNeil Falls. She is the lightest-colored bear seen within the sanctuary in many years, a trait passed along to her cubs.

Only recently has the breeding season peaked and begun to wane. For over five weeks, the big male followed the scent trails of several females in the area and eventually mated with a few of them. Now, after subsequent days of grazing on the intertidal sedge flats, this dominant male has arrived to claim his midsummer fishing spot. Twelve years he has fished at these falls, and for the last three years he has dominated the best location. Few bears can match his size, strength, and aggressive demeanor, and except for one or two other big males, all bears move away from him when he approaches.

The bear on the midstream rock, who was first on the river this morning, has temporarily had his fill and, with head on paws, is stretched out asleep. He is not as big as his neighbors, but he still weighs more than five hundred pounds and by fall, after fattening on fish and berries, may weigh over eight hundred pounds. The noisy gulls that surround him and hover in the air above the river don't seem to disturb his rest. Yet somehow, when a female and two yearling cubs troop down from the alders on the south side of the river, he is on his feet and watching their approach to the falls.

Flanked closely by her cubs, the female walks directly to the river and takes up a position opposite the watchful bear on the center rock. As she nears the river, the male's enormous head droops low, making his shoulder hump seem even bigger than before. Once the female begins to search for fish, the male lies back down on the rock, but this time facing the family.

The female is well-furred, a sharp contrast to the thin coats of the males. Her fur is long, perhaps five inches in places, and coarse. The guard hairs are bleached by the sun and lighter than the dense, tightly woven dark undercoat. She is straw-colored, while her cubs who huddle nearby wear dark coats. After several minutes she catches her first fish, and before she can turn completely around, the cubs are running toward her for a share. She dashes between them, knocking one down, and climbs the bank where she quickly tears the salmon apart and bolts down the chunks. She does not share, and in her hunger keeps her cubs from the fish. As she turns back to the river, the cubs growl loudly over the gill plates, tail,

Bears are omnivorous, with plants often providing the bulk of their dietary needs. Horsetail, also known as equisetum, is a favorite food that grows well in moist soils.

and paltry scraps. As the afternoon wears on and her hunger abates, she tolerates her cubs' aggressive demands, and they steal ever larger portions of her catch, eventually wresting a whole fish from her.

By late afternoon perhaps as many as twenty bears have come and gone, and the grouping peaks at around fifteen. Two females, each accompanied by two yearling cubs, fish the south bank, while another female, this one with three two-year-old cubs, fishes the north side of the river, but well downstream from the four big males who dominate the activity on that side of the falls.

Young males and females without cubs move around on both sides of the river, trying to find fishing sites not taken by the more dominant males and family groups. Often when these smaller, less dominant bears catch a fish, they run into nearby thickets to eat their catch in relative security. More than once a subadult bear has given up its fishing site to a more dominant bear. All that is needed is a close approach by a dominant bear or a family group, and the subordinate bear backs away. Once a mature female swatted a subadult male that at first would not yield to her, eliciting a cry of protest clearly audible over the thundering river.

Bears are usually solitary animals, and they are only drawn together here by their hunger. Generation after generation of bears has brought cubs to these falls. The young learn not only how and where to catch fish, but how to cope with other bears. Only where food is concentrated do bears congregate and exhibit this tolerance for one another.

Kamishak country is characterized by wind, rain, and cool temperatures. Even on a sunny day the sedge flats and mountain peaks can be buffeted by high winds.

Subtle and overt messages are exchanged between bears, and these signals dictate the flow of action. There are no females with cubs of the year here now, but later in the summer when they do show up, a whole new dynamic will be added to the scene. Just ten days from now, more than fifty bears will crowd into this quarter-mile stretch of river at the same time. The salmon run will peak at several thousand, enough fish to support this, the world's largest concentration of brown bears.

McNeil, River of Bears, flows into Kamishak Bay, which lies west of the southern tip of the Kenai Peninsula and at the mouth of Cook Inlet. The wide, shallow bay is exposed to the tumult of the Gulf of Alaska. And above the ocean mists and clouds over the bay and this country of bears appear the crenelated summits of innumerable peaks.

"Mountains almost alive," one explorer said in awe when viewing the smoking crown of one. This snow-draped peak was Illiamna, a 10,016-foot volcano, whose summit fumaroles were first sighted by European explorers in the eighteenth century. It is one of the most northerly of about eighty volcanoes that form the Aleutian Arc, or the "Pacific Ring of Fire." The volcanoes Mount Illiamna and Mount Douglas stand as sentinels north and south of the bay, while Mount Augustine, forming its own island, sputters and fumes thirty miles offshore. Over time the Kamishak Bay region has been dusted by numerous ash falls including a smothering blanket from the 1912 Mount Katmai blast. In 1976, and then again in 1986, Mount Augustine erupted, followed by an eruption of Mount Redoubt in 1989–90. The Russians called Augustine Island *Chernaboura*, or "Black Storm."

The name Kamishak Bay is a corruption of the Russian *Guba Kamchatskaya*. (*Kamchatka* means "where the land ends"; *Guba*, "shallows," or "little water.") English seafarers entered Kamishak Bay as early as 1787.

Russian traders and hunters passed through the area, at least as early as 1796, when one of their trading vessels, *Tri Sviatitelia*, "Three Sisters," beached and was wrecked, with the loss of four lives, furs, and trade goods.

The Chigmit Mountains that encircle the bay were formed by the colossal impact of the earth's crustal plates and shaped by the relentless forces of volcanic fire and glacial ice. They are part of the mountain backbone of the Alaska Peninsula that sweeps west and south to the Aleutian Islands.

Here the earth is still restless. The Bruin Bay Fault lies just north of Kamishak and parallels the subduction zone. The ground not only infrequently rolls and shakes, but on occasion threatens massive reshaping. On March 27, 1964, the most severe earthquake ever recorded in North America shifted a fifty-thousand-square-mile area. In parts of southcentral Alaska the land rose as much as thirty-eight feet; in others it dropped seven feet; sections shifted laterally up to twenty-five feet. Rock slides and avalanches roared down from the highlands and into the sea. What was once covered by tides was left high and dry. Fissures opened in the ground. Seismic waves, tsunamis, crashed ashore thousands of miles away. Even now the west shore of Cook Inlet is a rising, emerging coastline.

The inexorable force of four Pleistocene glaciations shaped the mountains and valleys. Just north of McNeil River in what is a wink of geologic time, ten to fifteen thousand years ago, Pleistocene mammals roamed. The woolly mammoth, short-faced bear, stag-moose, saber-toothed cat, and lionlike cat shared the interior Alaskan steppe with antelope, horses, camels, Dall sheep, lynx, wolves, wolverines, and brown bears. Today brown bears still forage on the strand while volcanoes steam in the distance above the cool ocean air.

Summers here, near 60 degrees north latitude, are short, cool, and rainy; winters are stormy, long, cold, and dark. Summer's longest day is a little more than twenty hours, compared to winter's shortest day of five hours. By late October, frost lies heavy on the land, with breakup coming sometime the following April. Snow and ice persist at sea level in some years until June. The growing season is short. A very few groves of deciduous trees take root in isolated pockets; a few scattered spruce, stunted and twisted like bonsai, struggle against the wind and cold. Despite the long summer days, only grass and alders seem able to flourish. Some years even the wildflowers fare poorly.

Can a more dynamic shore exist? One under assault from erosion and volcanic upheaval, freeze and thaw, tide and wave, torrent and tremor. A place where bears stalk the strand lines as they have throughout the ages.

All over the world, wildlife continues to disappear at an alarming rate as habitat is destroyed and animals are killed for food, profit, or from fear or ignorance. In Alaska, in this sanctuary, we have the chance to do things right and learn from the mistakes of others.

WHEN BEARS GO FISHING

A WALK TO THE FALLS ON MCNEIL River is always charged with a special mystery and magic. No matter how many times a person is privileged to make this two-mile jaunt, the anticipation, the excitement always quicken. Perhaps from camp a bear has been seen in the distance. This glimpse stirs the imagination.

Camp consists of three cabins, a sauna, outhouses, and a collection of small tents amid a field of tall grass and wildflowers. It is located two miles from the falls, in an area chosen not only because the alders offer a windbreak for the tents, but more importantly because its distance from the river ensures that the impact of humans on the bears will be minimal.

At midmorning sanctuary manager Larry Aumiller appears in front of the cook cabin. "Ready to go?" he quietly asks us, the assembled visitors. We answer with smiles, some nervous laughter, and a chorus of assent. He asks if everyone has lunch, raingear, and warm clothes and checks to see that each is wearing hipboots. He makes a joke about leaving cameras and film behind today because it might rain and the bears will be in raingear and not photogenic. It dispels the lingering tension, and the ten people fall into file behind him.

Soft-spoken and articulate, Aumiller is counterpoint to the often nervous, excited sanctuary visitors he guides. Bearded, tanned, and fit, this rather compact man has a pleasing, low-key manner spiced with a deep, infectious sense of humor. Often he defuses anxiety or tension with off-the-wall playfulness akin to cartoonist Gary Larson's. His low-key demeanor makes him the perfect "bear guide" for wildlife watchers, but friends know that under the carefree facade lurks an intense concern for bears in general and the sanctuary in particular.

A brisk pace leads onto the mudflat and soon to the Mikfik Creek crossing where everyone stops to pull up the tops of hipboots. The water will only be knee deep, but it is cold, and a dunking in the typically cool weather would spoil that person's day.

Left: *Seagulls fussing over fish scraps often attract bears, who claim the scraps for themselves.* **Inset:** *Ms. Mouse and her three yearling cubs successfully catch red salmon on Mikfik Creek. Cubs of all ages eat salmon.*

All across the flats, skeins of bear tracks loop from point to point but most head toward the mouth of the river. A large set of tracks, flanked by the smaller prints of two cubs, draws special attention. It is hard to believe that the makers of those tiny fox-sized tracks will one day grow to the size of the maker of the big ones. A woman places her booted foot neatly inside the outline of the track left by the mother bear's hind foot.

Our group ascends the bluff and follows a well-worn trail across the tundra and parallel to the river. It is good to be out of the clinging mud and onto solid footing. From the river, we can hear the cry of gulls and the dull, distant roar of tumbling water. Somewhere an eagle shrieks.

The trail skirts several alder thickets, and each time we pass near one, Aumiller yells a loud salutation—"Hey bear! Hello Bear!"—to warn any bears that might be resting or hiding in the alders. "We never want to surprise a bear," he explains. "This is our method of knocking at the front door. Just letting them know we are here."

Suddenly we stop, and like a cartoon troop of soldiers, the last person in line, who is gawking at the country, bumps into the person in front of him, who in turn rear ends the next, and she the next. Goofy chuckles give out when the stragglers see the bear crossing the trail in front of the column.

"He's huge," a woman whispers. "My first brown bear," the man at the rear of the line also whispers. He shakes his head slowly from side to side, as if he cannot believe what he is seeing.

The bear, actually an average-sized female, wanders by without displaying much interest in the people. A few human pulse rates might be stratospheric, but she seems barely awake enough to be ambulatory. In the typical pigeon-toed gait, she wanders over the bluff and drops out of sight into the river course.

"Whew, she was close," Aumiller quips. "Next time I'd better bring a real gun instead of this squirt gun." His joke breaks the collective breath-holding, and the group moves on. Within a quarter of a mile, the trail abruptly turns right toward the river. Now the roar of the falls is louder and more vibrant; the pace of travel becomes slow and deliberate.

The group comes to the edge of the bluff. The sound of the falls mixes with the cacophony of dozens of feud-

ing gulls. And there are bears. Everywhere. On the rock outcroppings in the river, on the near bank, in the grass on the bluff on the far bank, swimming or splashing in the river. It seems unbelievable, and each person makes a count. Twenty-eight brown bears.

There are big ones, little ones; adults, cubs, and family groups. There are light ones, dark ones; portly ones and lanky ones. All intent on fishing. Even now some are eating salmon. And, more amazingly, except for one that ran away on the far side of the river as soon as the group appeared, none seems to be paying the slightest bit of attention to us.

"Just a few words before we head down to the pad," Aumiller says. "When we first get there, our impact on the bears will be the greatest, so stay quite close together at first and avoid fast movements or loud noises. After a bit, we can be a little freer in our movements since this is a spot where the bears expect to see us and find us.

"Throughout the day bears will be coming quite close, and likely more will be showing up later on. I'll take care of everything, you need not be concerned about anything but taking pictures or watching the activity. Welcome to McNeil River."

McNeil River bears are North American brown bears (*Ursus arctos*), a group that includes two subspecies, the grizzly bear (*Ursus arctos horribilis*) and the Kodiak bear (*Ursus arctos middendorffi*). Most scientists place the Eurasian brown bear in the same species.

In Alaska, quite arbitrarily, people commonly call coastal bears "brown bears," while interior bears are "grizzlies." Biologists make no such distinctions but instead lump the bears under a single heading, brown/grizzly bears.

There are several good places to see and watch brown bears, but nowhere is there an area that has a concentration of brown bears that even approaches that of McNeil River. Bears normally avoid one another, but because McNeil offers a combination of a rich source of salmon, and a geologic feature that makes that source readily available and easily caught, bears here have evolved a rather site-specific tolerance for one another.

Population densities throughout Alaska vary depending on the richness of the habitat. Dick Sellers, the biologist in charge of administration at the McNeil River Sanctuary, estimates the density of bears along the Katmai

Perhaps a visitor's first introduction to the sanctuary's bears is tracks lacing the tidal mudflats.

Despite the fairly typical weather, an excited group of visitors leaves camp headed for McNeil Falls.

Coast at about one bear per seven-tenths square mile. In contrast, the North Slope of Alaska, which can be snow-covered for eight months a year, supports but one bear per one hundred square miles. One estimate places the density of bears at McNeil during the peak of the salmon run at thirty per square mile. And although this figure does not reflect an annual density, it is incredible to realize that in summer over one hundred bears or more can be found within a mile or two radius of the falls.

Alaska, with an estimated thirty to forty thousand brown bears, supports about 99 percent of the total species population left in the United States and 75 percent of the North American total. Once one hundred thousand bears roamed the western United States. People with guns, traps, and poison, as well as habitat destruction brought about by logging, homesteading, and animal husbandry, quickly wiped out the brown bear over most of its range.

Brown bears are large, the record male topping fifteen hundred pounds. Adult females at McNeil River average four to five hundred pounds and adult males eight to nine hundred pounds, with an occasional giant of twelve hundred pounds. Brown bears vary in color

from blonde to chocolate. They have a pronounced shoulder hump, short "dished" face, and thick claws from three to five inches in length. They are slow-growing, and long-lived, with low reproductivity. Females have small litters, skip several years between them, and may not produce cubs until eight years of age. Because of their extended denning periods, four to seven months each winter, brown bears are physiologically unique among large terrestrial mammals.

Male bears are commonly referred to by the public as "boars," females as "sows." Though traditional, these terms are more appropriately applied to swine and not to bears.

Brown bears are powerful, intelligent animals that rely on their keen sense of smell not only to find or avoid other bears but to seek out a variety of foods. Brown bears have excellent hearing and, contrary to popular belief, good eyesight. They inhabit a wide variety of terrains, from the rainforests of Alaska's southeast Panhandle to the barren lands of the arctic tundra. Such habitat diversity is possible because bears are omnivorous and eat plants, fruits, and meat, including fish. Over most of their range, brown bears often subsist mostly by

To preserve as much as possible the wilderness flavor of the sanctuary, the campground is minimally developed. Visitors must be self-sufficient campers.

grazing. A few individuals are adept hunters of moose and caribou calves, in some areas killing up to 40 percent of the entire spring production. Others are avid fish-takers, catching and eating as many as eight, or more, eight-pound chum salmon per day.

When bears first arrive at McNeil River, they are very hungry and may consume about 15 percent of their body weight in salmon each day. It is not uncommon to watch a newly arrived five-hundred-pound bear consuming seventy-five pounds of fish. Groucho, when he was eleven or twelve years old, was one of the largest, dominant males on the river. Once while fishing from a prime falls location at the peak of the salmon run, Groucho caught an astounding ninety-one salmon in one day. He couldn't eat all of his catch, of course, but many less dominant bears benefited from his castoffs.

McNeil River's "fishing bears" have become famous over much of the world. Photographs and movies, magazine articles, and books, such as Tom Bledsoe's *Brown Bear Summer,* have lured people from all over. Not satisfied to just see pictures or read stories, people want the chance to experience this impressive concentration. They want the unique opportunity to walk among the bears

and to observe natural behavior. Some people may even have heard hair-raising tales and come for the thrill. Most leave changed by their experience, their views of bears at least somewhat altered. Many for years afterward recount their own stories of bears named Goldie, Scarface, and Melody.

"The one thing that really stuck in my mind was the day Larry Aumiller led us up to Mikfik Falls. We encountered a bear named Regina there. I'll never forget her or that incident," recalls photographer Johnny Johnson.

"While she was still quite some distance away, Larry said, 'She'll give us a little rush when she gets closer.' Sure enough, ten minutes later, she put on this little charge, and Larry stepped forward and yelled, 'No!' Regina stopped still, then went on her way completely ignoring us thereafter. Larry looked at me, laughed, and said, 'They're so predictable.'"

"I don't believe it! It can't be possible!—but it is!" writes visitor James Miller of California. "To turn your back on a 1,000-pound boar eating a salmon 10 to 12 feet from you without a thought of fear to watch the twins, Blondie and Brownie, fight over a piece of salmon is unbelievable. To see Teddy stretch out to nap 20 feet

Above: *The viewing pad at McNeil Falls brings humans close to brown bears. Because human activity at the falls is restricted to quiet movements on the pad only, bears often pass quite close, sometimes as close as ten feet. From this site, sixty-seven bears have been seen at one time.* **Left:** *McNeil River flows out of the Chigmit Mountains into McNeil Cove. The campground (lower right) is located two miles from McNeil Falls (left).*

away is equally amazing. I knew about McNeil before I came here but was not prepared for what I experienced, observed, and felt. The perception the public has of bears is very inaccurate."

THE TRADITION OF NAMING BEARS GOES BACK AT LEAST TO THE mid-1950s but quite likely well before that. In 1953, photographer Cecil Rhode called one bear Mopey to reflect the bear's apparent lassitude. A year or two later, Steve McCutcheon, a pioneer Alaskan photographer born in Alaska in 1911, saw one so worn and raggedy he called it Patches. It seems humans cannot resist giving names to bears to help identify them.

Most of the names that bears acquired throughout the 1960s and early 1970s were keyed to their study collars or ear-tags: Red Flap, Green Collar, Red Stripe, White, and Olive Drab. A bear might also be known by ear-tag number or lip tattoo, such as 1818 (Olive Drab), but would never be called by that number. Then there were descriptive names like Romeo, Big Momma, Hardass, and Killer. Names were given that had nothing to do with the physical or scientific description of the individual bear: Charlie Brown, Arlo, Flashman, Ladybird, and Groucho, Harpo, and Chico.

Throughout Larry Aumiller's tenure at McNeil River sanctuary bears have been named not only for physical and behavioral traits, but also for the rare few people who have had a particular association with the sanctuary: McBride (for guide Mike McBride), Helen (for the late photographer Helen Rhode), and Sterling (for biologist Sterling Miller). Aumiller, however, seems to prefer names that are either descriptive of the bear or its behavior. A goofy cub was Wingnut, an untrustworthy female Jezebel, a male with a ragged coat Patch Butt, a handsome male Pretty Boy, and the self-explanatory Chaser, Weird, and Dismay.

"To avoid anthropomorphic connections bears shouldn't be named, but McNeil is different," remarks Jim Faro. "We need to communicate with the public as well as we can. Names are something that humans can quickly grasp. If we say this bear is 1713 and that one 1317, for example, the public isn't going to understand as fast as if we said that one is Spooky."

Jim Faro is a large man who seems to fit the country that bears call home. His trademark is an overflowing walrus moustache. He's a staunch defender of his opinions shaped through years of field work. Faro was the first wildlife biologist on the Alaska Peninsula and as such had few guidelines concerning the studies that should be undertaken. He learned through trial and error and set an example of diligence and hard work that his successors toiled and still toil to match and exceed.

"Sanctuary bears are named for several reasons," Aumiller adds. "First, to keep track of them as individuals. Second, we have a mandate in our management plan to maintain a certain minimum number of bears at McNeil. Names help us identify and remember individual bears. Next, we collect some research, especially reproductive information, through individual identifications. Last, the staff needs to know which bear is which, and to be able to describe individual behaviors to one another, to ensure visitor safety through uniform response to each bear."

Because visitors are restricted by permit to brief stays in the sanctuary, there is a compelling need for rapid education. Over the years, the type of visitor traveling to the sanctuary has changed. In the early years, most visitors were professional outdoorsmen—photographers, guides, biologists, or fishermen. On my first visit in 1975, of the nine people in attendance, all were either professional photographers or biologists. Until the late seventies, McNeil was accessible only by boat or expensive charter flights from Anchorage, King Salmon, or Homer. Kamishak Bay country in summer is windy, rainy, and cool, and consequently the visitors that turned up in the early years were usually experienced and well-equipped for wilderness camping.

"The type of visitor that we see now is very different than in the earlier years," Aumiller observes. "Following the publicity generated by the 1986 *National Geographic* television special and video, we began attracting older, less outdoor-oriented people and families. A few are merely 'vacationing,' and as a group are not very well prepared for the weather, the long hours of observation, and the rigors of a four-mile hike. Some don't even bring hipboots to wade the water courses or intertidal areas."

Visitation has increased from five in 1968, to a record 304 in 1988. In 1991, 1,818 applicants cast lots for the 140 permits. Over 1,700 applied in 1992 with winners coming from nineteen states and four foreign nations. Not surprisingly, there has been some pressure from the

Above: *Led by sanctuary employees Colleen Matt and Derek Stonorov, a group of visitors spots a bear feeding on the sedge flats.* **Right:** *Restrictions on human activity allow bears unimpeded access to the river and freedom from human competition for fish. All access to the sanctuary is by permit only.*

NO
SPORT FISHING
BEYOND
THIS POINT

Above: *Almost every first-time visitor to McNeil State Game Sanctuary has heard all the scare stories concerning bears and brings along at least some anxiety. Most visitors learn that the only thing in life humans really need to fear is ignorance and prejudice.* **Right:** *Rusty, an adult male, begins to eat a salmon that he has just caught. Bears have surprising dexterity with their claws.*

Above: *Early in the season, hungry bears eat every bit of the salmon that they catch—or steal—from other bears.* **Right:** *Bears employ a variety of fishing techniques. Here a young bear tries to pounce on a salmon encountered in the shallows below the falls.*

Bears often pin their catch to the ground before eating it. The eggs, skin, and portions of the head are the preferred parts of the salmon.

public to increase the number of people allowed into the sanctuary, either by increasing the number of permits or shortening the time periods awarded lucky permit holders. Most proposals to increase visitation have been rebuffed, primarily for safety reasons, but also because large groups tend to change bear behavior. A few years ago, in order to accommodate increasing demand for permits, the duration of each permit was cut to four days. Some changes in the system are anticipated.

Since the late 1960s, the Alaska Department of Fish and Game's employees stationed at the sanctuary have played a huge part in not only protecting the bears but also enhancing human safety and enjoyment. Many visitors leave enthralled with bears and sanctuary staff.

Jim Faro deserves immense credit for directing a great change in the role that human visitors play in the sanctuary. People have become more unobtrusive, their presence almost neutral.

Larry Aumiller marked 1992 as his seventeenth consecutive summer as sanctuary manager. He has become recognized as an authority on sanctuary bears and their behavior. He is also a strong defender of the sanctuary and stresses the importance of maintaining the quality of what has become known as the "McNeil experience." He shares Faro's philosophy that it is better not to see or experience some unique wild area than to see it in a diminished state caused by an effort to accommodate large numbers of people.

"I hesitate to think what might have happened at McNeil River had we crammed in as many people as possible. We'd never have known what we'd lost," Faro observes. "Protection of the concentration of bears and quality of the experience should continue to be the prime management goals of the sanctuary in the future."

Aumiller's attachment to the sanctuary has been at times labeled obsessive because he lives another of Faro's precepts—the bears come first. Somehow, without risking the bears or people, he finds ways to satisfy and enrich the experience of both the demanding professional photographer as well as the most apprehensive visitor. As is true with all wildlife management, the real task at the sanctuary is people management.

So many people are instilled with distrust, even fear, of bears, that one of the important tasks of sanctuary personnel is visitor education. Aumiller feels that it has been very helpful through the years to have a woman on the staff to help with visitor education. It is his opinion that the presence of a woman allays a lot of uneasiness about bears that many first-time visitors share, the macho and gentle alike. It sends the message that a person need not be hairy, have knuckles that drag the ground, nor carry a nuclear cudgel to be safe at McNeil River.

Over the last seventeen years, four employees have made special contributions to the sanctuary, each in a unique way, above and beyond bureaucratic requirements. In the mid-1970s, Maureen "Mo" Ramsey's irrepressible brand of Australian humor helped define the low-key manner that still characterizes sanctuary employees. She was not a biologist or a scientist, but she could help relax even the most jittery visitor. When asked about the ammunition that she carried in her shotgun, for example, she would quip, "Bullets? We don't carry bullets. They're too bloody heavy!" Puzzled visitors quickly would catch on to the joke, learning that their visit was not life threatening.

In the early and mid-1980s, seasoned biologist Polly Hessing began collecting expert notes on bear behavior and helped to catalog descriptions of each bear. Thanks to Hessing's tenacious and meticulous note-taking, subsequent employees following her lead are able to keep track of individual bears from notes like "350 pound female, scar on left shoulder, white claws. Does not approach people or upper falls, about eight year old." Polly's easygoing manner and incisive humor kept visitors comfortable in all situations and in all weather conditions.

Colleen Matt spent eight years as a youth camp director, naturalist, and backcountry ranger in several national parks in Alaska before coming to work at the sanctuary in the late 1980s. She had recently worked at nearby Katmai National Park where she became fascinated by bear interactions with humans as well as other bears. She described her time at McNeil River as being "like a graduate school and a Disneyland for animal behaviorists." Her enthusiasm for observing wildlife rubbed off on visitors.

Derek Stonorov worked as a graduate student at McNeil in the early 1970s, prior to the current bear watching program. He returned to work at the sanctuary in 1990. He was surprised to find that both the number of bears and their comfort with human proximity have increased since his early days as a researcher. Humans are allowed to see "bears just being bears," he says, more now than ever before due to the bears' increased tolerance of humans. Because bears are less stressed by humans, they seem to play more and interact more than in Stonorov's early days in the sanctuary. His "historic perspective" is invaluable.

Having a woman on staff also offers female visitors personal support. "I'd guess that most women coming to the sanctuary express fear of bears' attacking menstruating women," Colleen Matt explains. "Nearly all ask the same question and share the same misconception. I tried to set visitors at ease about that fairy tale right away."

"The belief that menstruating women are at special risk in bear country," visitor Barbara Meyer admits, "always affected when and where I went camping. I certainly knew the story before I went to the sanctuary. It is a widely held belief and I'm glad to know it's an untruth."

Aumiller agrees that this concern is both widespread and unfounded. "It's asked at every talk I give," he said. He offers that dispelling such notions is just one reason why he thinks a gender mix is vital to the sanctuary staff.

In 1978, Chris Smith succeeded Jim Faro as area biologist in charge of administration at the sanctuary. Smith faced serious budget problems. Both he and his successor Dick Sellers worked toward making the sanctuary financially self-supporting. Sellers is a quiet man in his mid-forties. He is of average height but powerfully built, suggesting time spent both out-of-doors and in the gym lifting weights. He has been the area biologist for the Alaska Peninsula for over ten years.

Both Smith and Sellers tried to refine the permit system to avoid adverse impact on the bears and to improve visitor experience. Sellers has opposed land disposals south of the sanctuary which would negatively impact the bears, and has worked mightily to minimize conflicts with commercial fishermen who work near, and sometimes in, the sanctuary, "These year-to-year problems are not unsolvable, but it does take work and cooperation to ensure the protection of the sanctuary."

Above: Helen and her spring cub have just captured a very ripe female chum salmon. Eggs spurting out under the weight of Helen's foot will be eagerly devoured. **Right:** Scraps of fish left by bears are soon scavenged by other bears, eagles, gulls, or ravens. Nothing is ever wasted.

THE CLASSIC MISCONCEPTION ABOUT FISHING BEARS MAINTAINS that they either knock the fish out of the water and up onto the bank with a powerful swat of a paw, or that they catch them with their "fishhook-like claws." Neither belief is correct.

Bears employ a variety of techniques in catching fish. At McNeil Falls, the primary technique is simple: A bear merely waits for a fish to try to swim or jump the falls, then pounces upon it. How an individual bear fishes involves several factors, especially the physical configuration of the fishing site. In most places in Alaska, as exemplified by lower Mikfik Creek, a bear typically runs back and forth, chasing fish in the shallows until it catches one. The bear pins the fish with its front feet and picks the wriggling creature up with its mouth. Water level, location, and magnitude of the salmon run affect both fishing technique and success.

Sanctuary bears also catch an occasional jumper in midair. "One time on Mikfik Creek, when the water was really high," Aumiller recalls, "the fish were jumping at the falls like little rockets. Two bears sat at the top of the falls, snapping at fish as they were flying by. Snap right, snap left. Dinner out of the air."

Bear paws, for several reasons, work as quite effective tools for catching fish. "First, they are attached to several hundred pounds of bear," Aumiller explains, "which means there's a lot of weight and strength behind them. Bear paws are broad and rough-surfaced, ideal for holding a slippery, struggling fish. Then, of course, each paw has five thick claws which help pin the fish to the ground. They look like they'd be clumsy, but they are very useful and can be manipulated with a surprising degree of dexterity."

Most bears stand on the rocks or in the shallows, waiting for salmon to appear out of the foaming water. A few splash about like children at play in a pool. Given the right circumstance, all bears will steal fish from subordinate bears. To avoid such confrontations, some subadult bears prefer to carry their fish away from the river before consuming them.

Visitors are often surprised at the delicacy with which bears use their claws. I once saw a bear try to shake the water out of its ear, then insert a single claw into its ear and gently scratch at the irritation.

A bear's excellent sense of smell, good close-range vision, and dexterity of lips, tongue, and claws allow amazingly delicate and precise feeding habits. Some bears commonly use a single claw to remove eggs from a fish, as Aumiller describes. "After a bite behind the pelvic fins, just a very fine incision really, a single claw is inserted and the whole egg sack pulled out. As the eggs ripen—a female chum has three thousand of them—the eggs almost spill out on their own. As the fish becomes ready to spawn, all the bear has to do is push down with a paw and the eggs squirt out to be licked up. Eating eggs is a delicate operation, not unlike the way some bears daintily strip berries in the fall."

Late in the salmon run, once the eggs are stripped, bears often discard the rest of the salmon. It may appear to be a "waste" of the fish, but not so according to Jim Faro. "Discarded fish are frequently eaten by other bears, or by numerous gulls, eagles, and perhaps ultimately by the same bear when the run ends and only carcasses are left. By stripping the eggs, it appears bears are stuffing the limited volume of their stomachs with the highest caloric food item available. The rest of the salmon that washes downstream to be eaten by younger bears may make the difference in the younger bears' survival later on. Nothing is really 'wasted.'"

It is especially important to remember that bears eat for six to seven months in order to survive twelve. They must be choosy.

Age and experience also play a part in how an individual bear fishes. In general, the older and more experienced bears use less energy to catch fish than do younger bears. Efficiency increases with experience. It is rare to see large adults racing back and forth like the youngsters sometimes do when trying to catch fish. The dominant bears also get access to the best fishing spots by displacing smaller bears. The best spots are where bears can catch salmon with as little effort as possible. Some subadult bears are lucky just to sneak into the congregation at the falls and snatch a fish and run out again. Dominant bears, like the big male Dismay, control the best fishing sites and catch as many fish as are available.

Cubs learn how to fish from watching their mothers and by trial and error. They also cue into locations as well as techniques for coping with other bears. Lanky's cub Teeny, for example, fishes exactly in the same spot, if available, and with the same technique as her mother. The similarity is striking because not only do they physically look alike, they often even assume the same pose while fishing.

Cubs get all the scraps or whole fish that they can wrangle from their mother, but they are not fed directly. Cubs and hungry adults alike will take "floaters"—dead fish that get loose from other bears. Salmon that beach themselves draw quick attention.

Whether in response to the crowded conditions, or by accident, a few bears develop unique fishing techniques. "A bear we called Siedleman, who was named for a sportfisheries biologist," Aumiller explains, "had a rather unique style that no other bear has developed. It was site specific and likely developed quite by chance. He would go downstream from the center rock, put just his head under water, and lunge around. He'd actually submerge for up to a minute. It seemed that he was looking for fish as they swam by, and about one out of six times he'd come up with one."

Another bear, Mindy, would take a flying leap off the end of the center rock and belly-flop into the main pool in a riotous attempt to catch a confused fish. Another would dive to the bottom of the pool and bring up parts of, or whole, dead fish. It was astonishing to see a bear, hind legs kicking like a frog, disappear out of sight at the bottom of the twelve-foot-deep pool. Ladybird would throw herself in the shallow water on the far side of the river, splash a salmon out of the water and onto the bank, then catch it before it wriggled back into the river. These are extreme examples of variations in technique. Most bears generally fish more alike than not.

Some attempts at fishing are quite comical. "Early in the spring several years ago on Mikfik Creek," Aumiller recalls, "we were watching two bears grazing on sedges. Until then, there apparently had been no fish in the creek, at least we'd not seen any caught. The tide started coming in, and we noticed a small school of fish head up into the shallows.

"One of the bears, a little guy about four or five years old, heard the splashing. He was about sixty or seventy yards from them and couldn't see the fish; he stood up, cocked his head to the side, and stared into space for the longest moment. He probably saw the bald eagles starting to swirl around and swoop down on the salmon. It was their first fish, too. Finally realization sank in, and the bear was off at a dead run. He was so excited, he was tripping over himself coming down the bank.

"Mud and water went flying as he flung himself

down onto this little group of about ten or twelve salmon. He landed with legs outstretched, like a football tackler, and fish squirted into the air in all directions. Five or six beached themselves. Eagles were swooping around, and another got a fish. The salmon were spread over about ten feet of bank. He practically turned himself inside out in leaping toward them. He grabbed one, then seeing the next one, dropped the first, then grabbed the second one. He saw another, so dropped the second fish and grabbed the next. Then seeing yet another, he dropped the third fish and went after the fourth. Of course, fish were flopping all over the place.

"The bear lay down on his belly and started reaching out left and right as far as he could to scoop the fish into his chest. An eagle dove and caught another salmon. The bear actually ducked as the eagle went over. The fish started getting away, so he made another effort to scoop them up. Pretty soon he had four or five fish held against his chest. He had a terribly wild, excited look on his face. Now what?

"Finally he raised his hindquarters off the mud and scooted his upper body and the ball of fish across the flat as far from the water as he could get and began to devour his bounty one by one."

Bears almost never eat every scrap of the salmon they catch. Bony parts of the skull, the lower jaw, the gill plates, and the intestines are usually discarded. Aumiller likes to remember "when Groucho caught his record daily total of ninety-one, I bet he actually didn't eat half the catch. It was the same sort of response to stimulus that you'd see with a cat chasing after a ball. There's nothing to be gained nutritionally, but it's his instinct to catch those fish that come up in front of him. An innate reaction to which he has very little choice other than to respond."

The salmon caught by bears can be divided into prespawners and postspawners. Depending on the hunger of the individual bear, a postspawner may be discarded by a bear almost as soon as it is caught, without much besides the head being eaten. Late in the summer, after many bears have wandered out of the sanctuary, dead and dying salmon are sought by a number of bears, mostly females with cubs and subordinate bears that have avoided the falls. Some bears dredge the river bottom or scavenge the sandbars for putrefying and hardly recognizable fish remnants. Somehow even these grotesque

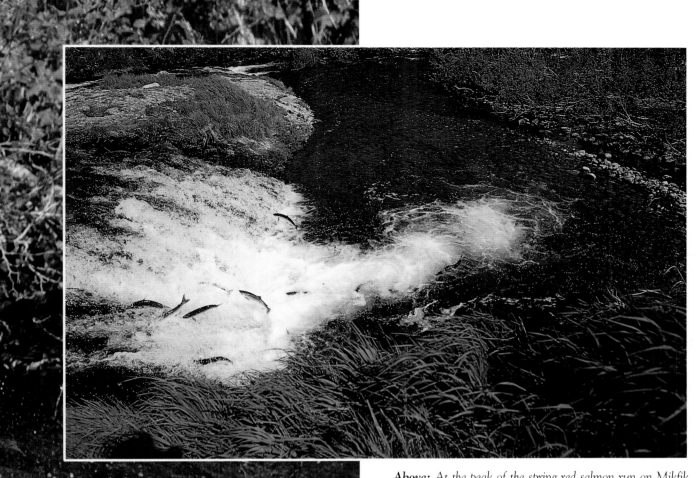

Above: At the peak of the spring red salmon run on Mikfik Creek, several hundred fish crowd the pool below the lower falls. One by one they'll work their way up and over the cascades and through the shallow stream to the lake at its head. Bears gather at the falls and along the water course for their first taste of fish after the long winter. **Left:** White and her cubs try to catch a jumping red salmon on Mikfik Creek. Cubs in their third summer of life actively fish.

cadavers have some nutritional value.

"McNeil River might be one of the very few places where bears catch prespawners," Aumiller explains. "At other streams in the area, and at places like Brooks River, the majority of the fish taken are postspawners. Perhaps the big draw at McNeil, and why bears bypass other streams to congregate here, is the access to the fish eggs."

Most bears are primarily crepuscular in their habits, their activity peaking in morning and evening. McNeil bears are an exception. Although there are bears present in the morning hours, activity builds throughout the long daylight of the Alaskan summer, peaking about ten or eleven o'clock at "night," well before dark. Intolerant bears, mostly large males, fish the falls early in the day and usually leave when people show up. Twice Faro stayed at the falls all night with a starlight scope and saw no bears fishing in the dark hours. Aumiller also found that bears did not fish in the darkest hours.

The magnitude of the salmon run is the key to maintaining concentrations of bears at the falls. The year 1989 recorded the fifth consecutive sizable run, but the next two years were dismal. Although in each of these two years, the same number of bears visited the falls, in 1991 use dropped 30 percent. Essentially the same numbers of bears arrived at the falls but spent less time fishing due to lack of fish. Additionally, in 1991, observers saw very little play behavior among the bears.

Nutritional needs must be met and without fish to catch, bears do not take long to move to other areas. It is unclear if fall foods alone—berries, carrion, silver salmon—can make up for any deficiency brought on by the failure of the summer salmon runs.

Biologists are reluctant to draw a direct link between summer fish runs and brown bear productivity, overwinter survival, and population density. "Although we can't demonstrate the link scientifically," Aumiller explains, "we could infer that the summer runs are very important for no other reason than the tremendous weight gains we see in bears. Waldo, for example, who is a medium-sized and -aged adult male, arrives at between 550 to 600 pounds and a month later leaves at 650 to 700 pounds. White arrives at 350 pounds and gains 100 pounds. Bears feeding at McNeil Falls gain an estimated 20 percent of their body weight. That's a gain that has to have an impact on survival. Even the shy bears that arrive late in the season, and stay maybe just two to three weeks, also put on noticeable pounds.

"Young bears have potential to gain a lot of weight, older bears less potential. A bear that biologists weighed in spring at Black Lake tipped the scales at 250 pounds but in the autumn weighed 500 pounds, an astonishing 100 percent weight gain. In contrast, we see obvious signs of deterioration in old bears as exhibited by Goldie or Romeo, for example. They are gaunt, they have disabilities, they have cataracts in their eyes. They don't catch many fish, and they don't put on much weight. If these old bears show up in midsummer in a gaunt condition, they just don't show up again the next year. They don't come back—and it's this gauntness that is the common trait of bears in their last season."

Dick Sellers is unwilling to say that these old bears die because they are unable to catch fish at McNeil, citing any number of causes for their demise. "I will speculate, however, that the summer feeding must be important to all bears because of the stresses they are under just to be there at McNeil River. Excluding some regulars, the stress within the concentration of bears at the falls is quite high, especially for younger females and females with cubs."

Sellers cautions that the year-to-year fluctuations in salmon numbers, while important, do not play a predominant regulatory role in bear population levels on a local scale. "For small areas like McNeil, there are major complicating factors like magnitude of the salmon runs in adjacent streams, alternative foods like berries and carrion, as well as bears that are killed by licensed hunters or by people defending their life or property. Fish availability is crucial for maintaining a high concentration of bears over the long term, but in the short term, bear numbers at McNeil have remained high even in years of poor salmon runs."

Alaskan brown bears, the giants of their race, in part have been able to attain their prodigious bulk because of the availability of rich sources of summer protein. Our challenge at McNeil River is to balance human desires with bear needs. The human desire to see bears is whimsical, but bears need the sanctuary for survival. The management plan for the sanctuary addresses this issue simply: "The bears come first."

Catching a lively and slippery salmon in fast water can be tricky business even for an eight-hundred-pound bear. People travel from all over the world to view McNeil River's famous "fishing bears."

WEST OF BLACK STORM

How the people of Alaska arrived at the decision to create a sanctuary where "the bears come first" is a story that can begin with the naming of the McNeil River. "Charles McNeil occupies a comfortable log cabin near the mouth of McNeil River," geologist Kirtley F. Mather reported during his 1923 exploration of Kamishak Bay. Mather described the region as mostly uninhabited and referred to the cabin as "McNeil Ranch." This was the first written use of the name, McNeil River, even though McNeil himself didn't seem to use it. As late as 1921, he listed his residence as "the mouth of the Little Kamishak River."

Charles H. McNeil quite likely built his home at the mouth of McNeil River rather than elsewhere in Kamishak Bay because of several factors, not the least of which were access to salmon, a shorter route to his mining claims, easier ocean access, and protected moorage behind the spit in McNeil Cove.

A few sources list McNeil as a "rancher" or "homesteader," but in reality he was a prospector. Born in LaCrosse, Wisconsin, in 1859, McNeil was not a young man when he came to Alaska. He apparently began to explore the area around Kamishak about 1904. In April 1910, he obtained a $1,250 grubstake, which entitled his benefactor to a fractional share in any and all mining properties and townsites that he might develop in Alaska. He was fifty-two when he filed his first claims in June and August of 1911.

As a prospector, McNeil was a little late coming into the country. The best mineral strikes were north and closer to tidewater. With his claims far from shore, in an area devoid of timber that mining then required, McNeil worked the fringe.

McNeil also worked as a stream guard for the U.S. Bureau of Commercial Fisheries. He trapped fur animals and shot seals. As "stream watchman," he monitored the salmon runs on local drainages. Along with Mr. Studdert, he built a "sluice" with rock and sod wings to funnel salmon up and over the tiny falls on Mikfik Creek. This

Left: In June brown bears gather on the tidal flats to graze on sedges, the first abundant spring forage plants available to them. *Inset:* Red salmon moving up Mikfik Creek in early spring attract bears.

The sanctuary campground is located well away from the sedge flats, Mikfik Creek, and McNeil River in order to separate humans and bears and allow bears unfettered access to these important feeding zones. The bears come first at McNeil.

crude fish "ladder" worked, and was still working in the early 1930s. McNeil watched as 175 red salmon an hour entered the stream during the five hours of each high tide. (In 1932, the Bureau of Commercial Fisheries permanently altered Mikfik Falls, not McNeil as is erroneously believed by some people.) McNeil also wanted to blast a fish ladder into the cascade at the mouth of Paint River, but was denied permission when it was learned that he demanded exclusivity to the proposed salmon run.

McNeil was in and out of Alaska. Some years he would overwinter, and others he would travel back to Ridgeway, Colorado, or to California. On December 23, 1924, he married Etta Kennedy in Atascadero, California, where they settled into chicken and fruit ranching on land she purchased in 1915.

Sunny California and a bride were a sharp contrast to the tundra and the brown bears of the windy Alaska Peninsula. McNeil had spent the previous year trapping around Kamishak, a remote, difficult land- and seascape.

His old home on McNeil Cove was ninety miles from Seldovia, which is on the Kenai Peninsula, and accessible by gasoline-powered launches only when the weather allowed. Seldovia was seven or eight days' steamer journey from Seattle. After his marriage, McNeil apparently never returned to Alaska but did have his memories. He had bearskins and a large photograph of two "playing" bear cubs hanging on the wall. His "ranch" was largely abandoned by the early 1930s, and his claims eventually expired for lack of assessment work. He died in Atascadero in 1948, at age eighty-nine.

What McNeil thought of the region's bears is unrecorded, but likely he didn't view them much differently than did other trappers and miners of the era. He probably thought that they were ubiquitous, but also dangerous. This was the era of the "Bruin Menace," a time when many in the territory viewed bears as "vermin" and favored their eradication. We do know that McNeil also saw them as a source of cash. In 1916, he sold bearskins to pay grubstake debts. Again in 1917, he

48

Charles H. McNeil hunted bears and seals, and trapped fur animals in part to pay off debt incurred from his mining enterprise.

paid off debts by trading in bear skulls and -skins. That year he had cash advanced by his charter boat operator on the purchase of four bearskins. In 1918, he received a total credit of $69.75 for ten bear skulls and also sold four bearskins. Two skulls collected by McNeil are in the United States Biological Survey collection in the Smithsonian. Just prior to leaving Alaska for good in late 1924, he obtained export permits for two brown bear hides.

Ironically, the world's preeminent bear sanctuary takes its name from a river named after a man who hunted bears for their hides and skulls in order to pay off a portion of his mining expenses and debts.

NO ONE CAN SAY HOW MANY BEARS FREQUENTED THE LAND drained by the McNeil River prior to the coming of Europeans, but it is safe to say that Alaska Natives did not impact the bear population to any great degree. Russian traders probably had little need to hunt bears in Kamishak since the Russians already were based on Kodiak Island, which still supports a healthy bear population. Itinerant prospectors often shot and killed bears, but in the Kamishak Bay area, such impact was likely negligible.

Anecdotal evidence indicates that there were not as many bears around McNeil in the early 1930s as there were in the mid-fifties. "Because there were no alders in those years, you could see a bear five miles away," recalls Steve Zawistowski who, beginning in 1932, spent twenty years fishing in Kamishak Bay. He said that the old timers believed that the dense alders now common there didn't take over the country until after the ashfall from the Katmai blast in 1912. Only after the alders choked the hillsides did the bears seem to increase.

Perhaps wanton killing held the bear population in check then. "Fishermen would shoot every bear they saw," recalls Zawistowski, "and bragged about the numbers at the end of the season."

Why? "For the same reason that former Governor

Overleaf: *Cubs, even yearlings like this one, often seek out physical contact with their siblings. This contact seems to reassure and relax them, especially when they're in stressful situations.*

'Eagle Bill' Egan hunted bald eagles for bounty . . . they ate fish!" adds Steve McCutcheon, a former deputy marshall and territorial legislator. "They were viewed as competitors. Fishermen were in the habit of slaughtering bears." Clem Tillion, himself a fisherman and guide, remembers one fisherman who "put a bullet in every bear he saw and often never followed them up."

The federal government, and later even the state, placed a bounty on almost everything that ate fish, or that was considered a "predator." These included bald eagles, hair seals, sea lions, dolly varden char and rainbow trout, wolverine, wolves, and coyotes. "Alaska will never make progress," one early territorial governor said, "until we eliminate brown and grizzly bears." Alaska Department of Fish and Game biologist Jim Faro found evidence that at some point in history "coyotegetters"—cyanide setguns—had been placed along McNeil River, obviously to kill bears.

"We started to see more bears over there in the mid-fifties after the territory started posting stream guards," Zawistowski recalls. Presumably the stream guards discouraged fishermen from shooting bears.

Through the 1930s and into the mid-1940s, Kamishak remained a hard-to-reach destination. Photographers and sport hunters were rare. After World War II, with veterans returned home and small planes increasingly available in Alaska, more and more people began to visit McNeil River. Some were hunters, and a few were photographers. In the late 1940s, the late Slim Moore, considered the "dean" of Alaska's fair chase guides, stopped at McNeil while traveling down the peninsula by boat on an extended hunting foray. His group killed two bears. One was killed by an assistant when it ripped into a wall tent that served as the kitchen. Later Moore was quoted as saying, "After going there, I didn't think it right that those bears should be hunted. It didn't seem sporting." He never hunted McNeil again and in the mid-1950s argued for protection.

Word of McNeil River's unique concentration of bears spread in the early 1950s. A few people began working toward special status for the area. In 1952, cinematographer Cecil Rhode, who had filmed wildlife for Walt Disney, and his partner Dick Chace, went to McNeil River for two weeks to make sixteen-millimeter motion pictures for the United States Fish and Wildlife Service. They were flown in by Cecil's cousin Clarence Rhode,

who was then the Alaska regional director of the federal Fish and Wildlife Service, as well as the executive director of the Alaska Game Commission and a promoter of the area as a "reserve."

Two or three bears were killed by hunters in the fall of 1953, and the area seemed to be under increasing hunting pressure.

Cecil Rhode's August 1954 article in *National Geographic*, entitled "When Giant Alaskan Bears Go Fishing," was one of the few articles ever printed by the magazine that did not give the location. "The author does not identify this river, lest hunters invade one of the animal's few remaining sanctuaries." Rhode's article pointed out that although bear hunters brought thousands of dollars to Alaska, "the bear alive is worth infinitely more to the photographer and nature enthusiast."

Rhode reported that the bears "settled right down," posed little danger to people, and if bothered crossed to the opposite side of the river. His group voluntarily stayed on one side of the river, leaving the other side to the bears.

In July 1953, Steve McCutcheon, having heard of the area from Cecil Rhode, arrived by boat for a photographic stay. "The first morning we were there, the fog began to lift and out across the flats and hills we could count seventy bears all at the same time," he recalls. It was the first of four trips McCutcheon made to McNeil in the mid to late 1950s. By this time, what had once been extensive natural grasslands had been largely taken over by dense stands of head-high alders.

McCutcheon remembers being a little on edge during the first part of his two-and-a-half-week trip. "I was a little nervous to begin with, but I learned right away that the least dangerous of all animals is a bear full of fish. In just a couple of days, I relaxed because I saw right away not to be afraid. In all the years I was there, no one ever fired a shot and we never lost anything to a bear." McCutcheon and his peers wrote letters to the United States Congress and territorial agencies, recommending that the area be closed to bear hunting.

In response to the growing pressure for protection, in 1955 the entire drainage was designated the McNeil River Reserve and was closed to bear hunting by order of the U.S. Fish and Wildlife Service and Alaska Game Commission. Cecil Rhode visited McNeil again in 1955. He offered perhaps the earliest written record of bear

The first physical sign of low-level stress is often an abbreviated yawn, as Helen demonstrates.

Although only ten feet by twelve feet, the campground's first cook shack, built in the 1950s, provided visitors with a sheltered place to cook and eat.

Above: *The campground structures currently in use were built in 1982. Sanctuary personnel live in this cabin, which replaced an older, smaller shack.* **Right:** *Norma Jean stands near McNeil Falls with her two spring cubs. All three watch the approach of another bear. Females with cubs are intolerant of the close approach of large males.*

concentrations at the falls: "Up to 32 have been seen at one time congregated for the feast."

"This spring the Alaska Game Commission, realizing the great potential of the locale for bear study, photography and tourist attraction, closed the immediate area to bear hunting," Rhode recorded in an unpublished magazine article, "thereby protecting and preserving for the future what is one of the world's most unique wildlife spectacles."

Rhode also described the bears' mild curiosity about people. He wrote of the few that exhibited an extraordinary tolerance of people as well as the species' general overall lack of aggressive behavior.

"In my two summers on the river totalling 85 days," Rhode continued, "I probably saw several hundred browns brushing awfully close to some of them, but only one gave me a bad scare." This was a bear that followed Rhode, "growling every step," for a hundred yards or so before turning off into an alder patch. Others had come closer. His experiences ran counter to the popular myths that persist even now, casting grizzly bears in the role of wanton killer of people.

Two years after the McNeil River Reserve was established, the U.S. Fish and Wildlife Service assigned its first "enforcement patrolman" to the area. Ivan L. Marx stayed at McNeil most of the summers of 1957 and 1958, living in one of two tin shacks that were built near the site of the present camp. He guarded the river from "creek robbers," fishermen who put their nets in the river and took all the salmon. He prevented poaching and recorded bear activity and numbers.

The annual bear hunting season opened on the Alaska Peninsula on May 6, 1958, and immediately Marx recorded regular passage of low-flying aircraft looking for bears. "May 10. Two planes spotting bear today. They left this area when they saw me." Aerial spotting of bears, which was legal for hunters then, continued well into the next month. From his sparse written accounts, it is obvious Marx believed he was preventing poaching. "June 8. Planes still coming over to spot bear. None land. . . . Frank Glaser has been here since Friday and has seen how a man protects the bear here." (Glaser had just

Ten-year-old Zubin cools off after catching and eating several chum salmon. Sanctuary bears are named so that individual bears can be identified and tracked both during each summer and year after year.

Helen's spring cub licks its mother's snout, perhaps for a tasty morsel left over from a fish repast, or perhaps for reassurance.

One of White's spring cubs takes a dip in the sauna pond to play with the water lilies, which are in full bloom.

retired from the Fish and Wildlife Service after a lengthy career as a "predator control" agent responsible for killing wolves across all of Alaska.)

Marx also recorded attitudes about bears voiced by four skippers of fishing boats anchored in McNeil Cove. "The captain of each boat are [sic] strong against the bear: 'There should be a bounty on them,' 'Too many bear is death on salmon,' 'We don't want them to become extinct but we don't need many,' 'They kill too many salmon.'" These were typical comments and attitudes of the time. In a follow-up passage, Marx wrote: "A mother and two yearling cubs crossed the flats 100 yards from three of the boats at low tide. Good thing I was here."

As had visitors earlier in the fifties, Marx found "all the bears very tame, they do not run from me." In early August, biologist Robert Rausch visited McNeil and by air counted fifty-three bears congregated at one time in the vicinity of McNeil falls, the first "official" count.

Alaska achieved statehood in 1959, and all functions of the territorial government, including wildlife management, were transferred to the state. McNeil River Reserve was a thing of the past, but the new Alaska Board of Fish and Game designated it the McNeil River Closed Area. This status prohibited bear hunting. As was the case in territorial days, the entire area was still open to hunting of other species, trapping, mineral exploration, and homesteading or other land development.

Clem Tillion introduced legislation in 1967 to establish McNeil River as a state game sanctuary. Tillion, a commercial fisherman and guide, had considerable experience in the Kamishak Bay area.

"The legislation was introduced in part because I feared that if hunters wounded bears, the bears would end up hurting a photographer," Tillion remembers. "Although the area was not heavily hunted then—none of Alaska was in the fifties—there was still concern. Also I felt there should be a compromise for hunters and photographers. There should be some places you can go to just see the bears and not have to worry about them."

Another concern of Tillion's was the effect that homesteading would have on the land and wildlife: "I'm all for homesteading and using the land, but it should be near roads and access—in other words, in legitimate areas for development. McNeil was not one of those areas."

Tillion's House Bill 156, "an act establishing a certain area of the state as a state game sanctuary to be known as the McNeil River State Game Sanctuary," was passed by the state House on March 15, 1967, by a vote of thirty-two to two; only Willie Hensley and Frank See voted against. On April 1, 1967, the Senate voted twenty to zero for passage, and the bill was then signed into law by Governor Walter J. Hickel.

A strong coalition of guides, biologists, hunters, and photographers had fought and won the battle for sanctuary status that protected the bears.

"I wanted a place where bears weren't afraid of us," Tillion says. "McNeil River today is exactly what I had in mind when I sponsored the legislation."

THE NEW STATE OF ALASKA DEPARTMENT OF FISH AND GAME took management control of McNeil River in 1959 and began stationing personnel there in 1960. In the early years, biologists or technicians would stay but two or three weeks at a stretch, unlike today's months-long tour of duty. This presence during the summer has been maintained continuously since 1964.

The state's first intensive effort to tag and study brown bears got underway in 1963. The objectives were to obtain information on reproduction, sex and age composition, movement, and mortality. The study also offered the opportunity to develop new drugs and techniques for live-capture and marking of bears. During the first four years of tagging, 1963 to 1967, thirty-five bears, eighteen male and seventeen female, were tagged and released. (Eight bears died from the effects of the drugs, and one drowned while immobilized. "It is sufficient to say," one report states, "that we have had a few wrinkles to iron out." Mortality from drug overdose decreased dramatically as biologists perfected their techniques.)

Guided and unguided photographers and sport fishermen and -women arrived in ever-increasing numbers after statehood. Some were day visitors who flew in by floatplane; others came by air or boat and stayed for varying lengths of time. Many camped in a cave near McNeil's old cabin. Problems mounted as more and more people arrived to see the bears. Twelve photographers crowded the scene at the same time in 1966.

Numbers of bears congregating at the falls declined in the mid-1960s and stayed low through the early 1970s.

An aerial photo of the campground shows the limited extent of human development within the sanctuary.

Maureen "Mo" Ramsey sits on a summer's worth of the sanctuary staff's food and gear as the departing amphibious aircraft taxis for takeoff.

Just fifteen to twenty bears a day congregated at the falls on a typical day in the early 1970s. Perhaps in years of low salmon numbers, bears congregated on other streams that had more fish. Biologists offered other possibilities.

"It is also possible that disturbance caused by the high number of photographers tended to keep bears away from the river," wrote biologist Joe Blum. On the other hand, at least one biologist believes the tagging study may have contributed to the decline. "Bears are smart, it doesn't take long for a bear to avoid places where people are sneaking about and whapping them with dart guns." Visitors also complained about the huge, bright collars that ruined photography.

Throughout the 1960s, the state imposed no restrictions on visitors and people did as they wished. By today's standards, some fairly zany things went on then. One photographer set up a blind on the center rock at the falls. Sport anglers would walk out onto the rocks to have their pictures taken with bears in the background. More than once bears raided camps or tents, looking for food—one party lost a slab of bacon—or chased anglers until they dropped their fish. Airplanes landed and took off directly in the lower river.

Brown bears declined throughout the Alaska Peninsula in the mid-1960s, according to Jim Faro, who reviewed all the pertinent data. He attributes the cause to diminished salmon runs throughout Bristol Bay and Cook Inlet.

"Bears at the sanctuary reached all-time lows in 1965 and 1966," biologist Dick Sellers adds, "but it's hard to see a correlation between that decline and salmon numbers. McNeil had record runs in 1963 and 1964. It seems rather obvious that something else was causing the decline at McNeil then. Perhaps the tagging operation and the attendant mortality, coupled with unrestricted visitor use, caused the decline."

Regional bear populations did decline in the late sixties, with a dramatic decline coming in the early seventies. Sport hunters across the Alaska Peninsula, including areas surrounding McNeil River, killed record high numbers of bears in 1972 and 1973. Emergency hunting closures in 1974 and 1975 stabilized the situation, Sellers says. "Hunting contributed to the decline," he explains, "but did not cause the decline. Such events are the result of multiple factors."

With one exception, the years from 1965 to 1975 saw the worst salmon runs ever at McNeil River. As the runs recovered in the latter part of that decade, due to improved conservative fisheries management, bears, then enjoying greater protection, also began to increase.

"Bears would not have increased at the falls, or elsewhere, regardless of the controls we put on people there," Faro points out, "if we hadn't had more food in the streams. The more food, the more bears."

In 1969, Jim Faro, as part of his duties as Alaska Peninsula area biologist, was placed in charge of the sanctuary. Armed with more than the usual share of foresight, he would soon lead the sanctuary out of a worsening situation. People were becoming more of a problem than the lack of salmon.

Alaska law allows the killing of a bear "in defense of life and property." Only two bears have been killed in the sanctuary under this provision. In 1969, a female accompanied by two spring cubs was killed by a guide accompanying a photographic party. The two small cubs, including one female who was subsequently ear-tagged and released, likely did not survive.

Then in 1970, in what would later become a well-publicized event, a photographer shot and killed a female bear. "She was fishing and he crawled up to her through dense grass along Mikfik Creek," Faro recalls, "and when she saw this shape in the grass she charged. She probably thought that it was another bear. It was a classic case of mistaken identity. He thought it was a false charge and kept on taking pictures. He stood up and put a bullet into her. He didn't fire over her head first or identify himself as human. It was totally avoidable." Her yearling cub was later destroyed.

"Unfortunately, when a person is harmed by a wild animal," Faro wrote in a report, "the general public seldom considers the possibility that the injured person may have been at fault."

It was clear to Faro and his colleagues that before someone got hurt at McNeil or more bears were killed, something had to be done to remedy the growing abuses. Not only were the bears increasingly disturbed by human visitors, but these visitors aggressively competed for camping and photographic sites.

According to Faro's data, twenty-five photographic parties visited the sanctuary in 1970 for a total of 215 use-days. The previous year, just nine parties observed bears for forty-five use-days.

"Some bears were intolerant of the actions of some photographers," wrote biologist Lee Glenn, "and apparently abandoned the falls or fished only at night.

"Unrestricted public use . . . reached the point where it endangered those intrinsic values which attract observers and photographers."

Recognizing the special nature of the sanctuary, the Alaska Department of Fish and Game decided to end intrusive research there. The year 1972 was the last year of tagging and "hands-on" bear research, and only two bears were handled. The previous year an "intensive effort was made to remove most of the collars." It was also another summer of heavy visitation when "photographers frequently out-numbered bears at the falls." Twenty groups of visitors accounted for 165 use-days, the second highest on record. It was a year marked with numerous "bear problems."

"A little carelessness with food will go a long way towards encouraging a bear to become a camp terror," Faro wrote after the 1972 season. "Two groups of photographers did not heed advice about food storage and suffered losses. The culprit bear destroyed two tents and damaged two others. In a bear sanctuary I was forced to turn to a twenty-gauge shotgun and fine birdshot to dissuade the bear." *People* were the obvious problem, not the bear.

The situation could only get worse. Alaska's human population was booming, and increasing numbers of people, lured by films, books, television shows, and magazine articles, wanted to visit the sanctuary. Killing of bears in the sanctuary was intolerable. The prescient, strong-willed Faro waged an almost one-man public relations campaign to garner public support for limited access. "The world-famous sight of brown bears fishing at McNeil River falls could be lost," he wrote in *ALASKA* magazine in 1971. "Signs of decline of this unique natural phenomena are already evident. The culprit: unplanned and unregulated exploitation."

Bears can be seen almost anywhere in Alaska and over much of western Canada, Faro told audiences, but the one thing they couldn't see anywhere other than McNeil was the concentration of bears. "That concentration must be protected," he said, "for it truly is a world wonder."

Faro eventually obtained approval from the Alaska Board of Fish and Game for a permit system that would

Above: *Unlike many other animals, bears don't have set sleeping patterns but rather take short naps throughout the day and night.* **Right:** *One of the oldest bears currently using the sanctuary is Rusty, a male who is probably over twenty-five years old.*

limit and control humans within the sanctuary. The permit system regulating visitors went into effect in 1973. It proved to be the pivotal event that ensured the success of the sanctuary program in the almost two decades since.

At first, there were few limits to restrict where people with permits could go or how long they could stay at the falls or on the flats. Visitors were unescorted. Access to the north side of McNeil River was prohibited. The majority of visitors then were professional photographers, and most carried firearms as well as cameras.

Walt Cunningham was the first on-site employee hired by Faro to monitor the permit system. He stayed part of the 1974 season and all of the 1975 season. He enforced the camping and access rules and lectured people on safety. He is remembered for his obvious appreciation and respect for the bears.

Larry Aumiller replaced Cunningham in 1976. In the ensuing years, Aumiller has helped shape and refine the permit system. Since 1978, each visitor group is accompanied to the falls by a representative of the Alaska Department of Fish and Game. Visitors are not allowed to roam at will. Food is carefully stored, unburnable garbage and trash is flown out, sport fishing is restricted, and the trail to the falls has been rerouted to lessen impact on the bears.

"Restricting activity and access within the sanctuary was the most important initial change," Aumiller says. "We can trace the success of the program today to that change coupled with the limit of visitors to the falls to ten per day. More bears drifted into the tolerant group from the wary category as they saw that humans weren't so bad."

"Consistency of the management philosophy of the sanctuary," adds wildlife photographer Johnny Johnson, "ensures that year after year, the bears get the same messages and signals from people. Other places, like Katmai

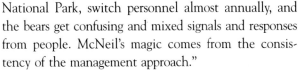

Above: *The aging Goldie, her vision hampered by cataracts, pauses in the afternoon sunlight of a day in the last summer of her life.* **Left:** *In the prime of life, two young bears test their strength in vigorous play.*

National Park, switch personnel almost annually, and the bears get confusing and mixed signals and responses from people. McNeil's magic comes from the consistency of the management approach."

It took a long time to undo some of the harm that occurred in the 1950s and 1960s. The number of bears started to increase about the time of the 1974 emergency hunting closures. It wasn't until the early eighties that bear numbers really took off.

Both Sellers and Faro point out that bear populations on the Alaska Peninsula have generally increased in recent years despite light to moderate hunting pressure. "Good sound wildlife management can provide bears for both hunters and viewers," Faro says.

Visitor Bart O'Gara, who made his journey to McNeil from Montana, expands on the biologists' view. "Such considerate, sensible, and sensitive management of a very unique resource should go a long way toward convincing many that hunters, and organizations supported by them, are indeed genuinely interested in the resource."

Aumiller feels that the sanctuary experienced a dramatic increase in the number of bears for two primary reasons: the long-term program that encourages use by bears, and a dramatic decrease in bear hunting around the sanctuary over the last ten years. In 1979, Katmai National Monument was extended north to abut a portion of the sanctuary boundary. State lands to the south between Katmai and the sanctuary were closed to bear hunting in 1985.

A rearticulation in 1981 of the management goal of the state of Alaska for McNeil River State Game Sanctuary stated that "Preservation of the unique brown bear *concentration* is (the State's) primary goal." Observation and photography of brown bears was listed as a priority use; scientific study a secondary consideration.

ON TRAILS
TWICE WALKED

VISITORS TO MCNEIL RIVER OFTEN bring with them a great deal of misinformation about bears. Each person's misconception about bears translates in varying degrees as either unreasoning fear or apprehension.

"Certainly any big furry animal that can bite you," Larry Aumiller admits, "can create apprehension, or fear. Danger. We're talking about danger, real or perceived, from an animate object."

Can the fear of bears always be explained in clear, rational terms? Or is it perhaps a more poorly understood phenomenon like the fear of snakes, heights, or the dark? Every human behavior cannot be explained away by calling it a "learned" response. More than one writer has theorized that our fascination with bears, a fascination that includes fear, may be one of the oldest connections known to humans, harkening back to the time when we lived in caves and warded off the terror of the night with bonfires. Perhaps the earliest evidence of religious expression was the arrangement of bear skulls and bones found in caves in southern Europe.

While it can be argued that part of our apprehension is innate, an argument can also be made that it is nurtured. We have, as one writer put it, "demonized" the bear through popular writings, scary stories, and barroom hunting yarns. We seem to need our ghost stories. For every balanced bear book like Thomas McNamee's *The Grizzly Bear*, a dozen others, like *Alaska Bear Tales*, only harm the image of bears through lopsided and often unsubstantiated reporting. "Most people have had little personal experience with bears," Aumiller observes, "and much of the literature is one-sided, emphasizing their danger and ability to inflict bodily harm."

Yes, today, on rare occasion, bears do hurt or kill humans, but for every instance of mayhem, perhaps thousands of other incidents end with a bear running in terror from people. These stories don't make headlines or good

Left: *Yearling cubs seldom wander apart when their mother leaves them to fish McNeil Falls.* **Inset:** *Two cubs rest on the cool sands of Mikfik Creek.*

leads for magazine articles.

Only two people have ever been hurt by bears at McNeil River, and neither incident can be construed as a "mauling." Considering the number of bears and their long-time proximity to humans in the sanctuary, the record is both astounding and illustrative of these bears' true nature.

"In 1955, a bear bit one guy on the foot," reported eye-witness Steve McCutcheon. "Just a bite. And that was because the fellow stepped on her."

Three years later, stream guard Ivan Marx described his run-in with a bear: "A large sow bear with new cubs charged me in the alders. . . . She started her charge at 20 feet so I three [sic] myself down on my back and lay still with my rifle pointed up at her chest. Al Hooker was running and trying to get his rifle off his pack and she forgot me. She ran across my legs and took after him. He fell down just as I started to shoot. At this instant she whirled and ran back over me to her cubs and reared up, then left. Either while grabbing at me or stepping on me, her claws cut a large gash in my knee, two of her claws went through my pants. My leg is stiff but I think I won't have to go to town." For at least three days afterward Marx was unable to venture far from the cabin.

"Marx got between a sow and her cubs, and when he saw this, he turned and ran, with the sow right behind him," Clem Tillion recalls. "He tripped and fell, and she ran right over him, her claws tearing open a nasty wound from knee to hip. But it really wasn't an attack, she was merely trying to get to her cubs. If he'd only stepped aside, she would have run right on by him."

Our readiness to believe outlandish stories of bears as "demons" who pose an absurd menace to humans is a by-product of our species' increasing detachment from the natural world. People inexperienced with wildlife so habitually look for a darker side to wildlife that they are bewildered when it eludes them. So many "bear chew" stories appear in popular literature and enliven oral reports that when confronted with the true non-aggressive nature of bears, some people are unwilling to accept this nature as reality.

"One of the real values of the sanctuary is that people can spend time very near to bears while not influencing bear behavior," Aumiller explains. "This allows people to see what real bears are all about. Not gruesome man-eaters or teddy bears. Bears are just bears. This realiza-

tion often creates a bond between people and the bear that they are watching. This can only help bears in the long run as people become supporters for bears and bear habitat. If enough people believe bears have a place in tomorrow's world, then perhaps bears will have a future."

Judging by visitor comments, some people do gain a new view of bears. "Growing up in Minnesota with black bears in my back yard, then later living in Montana near grizzlies, I actually viewed bears as merely overgrown teddy bears who were harmless," visitor Barbara Meyer told me. "Flying over McNeil Falls just before landing at the sanctuary, my eyes opened. This wasn't the open-air zoo that I had imagined. This was these bears' space, and they were in charge. I soon found out that I was there only because the bears let me be there.

"Since visiting the sanctuary, I now have an apprehension of bears. But it is a good apprehension. It is one of respect. Seeing a bear at a great distance, or viewing a black bear out the back window of the house, is entirely different than being surrounded by giant brown bears and seeing them up close. They are fluid, powerful, and sentient. I now enter their country—which is most of Alaska—with renewed respect, and appreciation."

LARRY AUMILLER TOOK HIS FIRST JOB AS FISHERIES TECHNICIAN with the Alaska Department of Fish and Game in 1972 and was stationed for part of the summer in King Salmon, a small community in the heart of the Alaska Peninsula. Often bears appeared in and around town, and Aumiller was anxious to see one.

Aumiller frequently went to the garbage dump near King Salmon to watch the bears that fed there. He met Jim Faro who at the time was the Alaska Department of Fish and Game area biologist. Soon he was volunteering to help Faro use a dart gun to immobilize and ear-tag bears. For the next four years, he continued to work on various state fisheries projects. While on stream surveys or at fish counting stations, Aumiller encountered a variety of different bears in a variety of situations. He also continued to volunteer his time to Faro's bear projects. He helped tag bears in Katmai National Park and spent two winters in King Salmon as Faro's housesitter and volunteer bear technician. In this capacity he estimates that he helped Faro dart and handle twenty-five to thirty bears.

In the late evening sun, Patches, a very old male, watches the water for any sign of movement. Older bears expend as little effort as possible when catching fish.

Left: *Some bears wander close to people by their own choice. Teddy will stop to eat her salmon catch quite close to people, sometimes within ten feet.* **Below:** *In late summer, spawned-out salmon often wash up on shore at low tide. Even these grotesque, sometimes putrid, remains provide repast for bears.*

From the McNeil Falls viewing pad dozens of bears can be seen at once. All sexes and ages are represented and sooner or later every behavior is seen.

Faro hired Aumiller in 1976 as the sanctuary's on-site manager. "I hired him because of his intelligence and his training. He also was likable and could deal with people.

"But most importantly, I felt that he would put the bears first, and that's what I wanted. He was given lots of freedom that first summer because I felt I'd given him the necessary background, now it was time for performance."

In the ensuing years, Aumiller has developed a remarkable ability to understand bears and is recognized as an expert on behavior. Faro takes this a step further: "Right now, his abilities at reading bears are the best in the world. No one does it better, and no one can do what he does."

Prior to his employment at the sanctuary, Aumiller admits to having had bouts of unreasoning fear of bears, which he calls "bearanoia." He recalls once staying up all night at a remote fish camp, with the furniture piled against the cabin door, expecting any second to have a bear come through the wall or door, much like monsters

do in those old B-grade movies. He laughs about it now.

Aumiller admits to going through three distinct phases, and blurred variations of them, as he has worked with bears and with people. "My original thought about the sanctuary was that here's a place with enormous potential for danger," he says, "and I was overly cautious and aware of the awesome responsibility of guiding visitors. I suffered from bearanoia. Then after four or five years came the regrettable cocky attitude that I'd seen it all and I knew what was going to happen. I don't think it really showed in how I did things, but inside I had a different perception and attitude.

"Now, after all these years, I'm in phase three. Every year there is something new, and it somewhat changes my view of what's been experienced before. I think if I watch long enough, I'll see everything eventually. It's a middle ground now. I'm very comfortable with our program of humans mingling with bears, and we certainly haven't gotten lax in terms of safety. That still comes first. An analogy would be skydiving, or any risky venture. The more you experience, the more you know the safety margins. With additional experience, the boundaries of knowledge of bear behavior can only widen. I guess I'm comfortable both with the bears and the responsibility."

BROWN BEARS LIVE MOSTLY SOLITARY LIVES. FIGHTING BETWEEN bears, except during the breeding season, is uncommon, if not rare. Actual combat has been noted in situations where the rewards to the attacker are high, such as during the breeding season or in unique food-gathering opportunities. Avoidance of conflict appears the rule rather than the exception.

Throughout much of the animal world, ethologists, who study animal behavior, say that ritualized displays take the place of aggression in order to minimize the possibility of injury to winners as well as losers. Threat and bluff are often all that are needed to establish dominance.

"Because adult bears have the power and weapons to kill one another, all successful bears readily communicate with a language of aggression and submission," writes Stephen Herrero in his acclaimed book, *Bear Attacks: Their Causes and Avoidance*. "Threat and appeasement signals have evolved because they reduce the incident of actual combat and the danger of injury to both parties."

Herrero points out that at unusual feeding congregations, such as at McNeil River falls, mutual avoidance behaviors, combined with a limited hierarchical organization, enable each bear to feed. Dominant animals, usually the largest or most aggressive, feed when and where they want. This social order both reduces the risk of injury and maximizes feeding time and opportunity. Research conducted within the sanctuary has clearly shown that instances of actual aggressive contact and injury are very low.

Why are bears sometimes aggressive? The reason, according to many sources, ultimately lies in the drive to achieve reproductive success. This holds true for both males and females. In northern, inland bear populations, females are unlikely in their whole lives to produce more than six or eight young, and not all of these reach sexual maturity. Each cub is crucial to its mother's reproductive success and is vigorously defended.

Females are scattered, never numerous, and receptive to breeding only every few years. Males do not defend a single female against all competitors over the course of the mating season but rather mate with as many females as possible. Even so, a male, while with a female during her brief estrus cycle, is sometimes pulled into dangerous contact with another male. When adult males fight over females, it is to help ensure that they will sire as many cubs as possible.

Ethologists explain aggression in animals outside mating season as being related to either food, territoriality, defense of young, or threat response. Derek Stonorov did his undergraduate thesis on the social behavior of Alaska brown bears, based on his work in 1967 and 1968 at Becharof Lake on the west side of the Alaska Peninsula. As a graduate student, he continued his study of bear social behavior at McNeil River in 1970 and 1971. He explains aggression this way: "Brown bears may become dangerous when what I prefer to term their 'individual distance' is encroached upon."

"Individual distance" can be defined as that distance around an animal that, if violated, will cause that animal to fight or flee. Stonorov points out that "individual distance" is just that: It varies from bear to bear and situation to situation. The response zone around a female with cubs, for example, depending on the female, usually is much larger than around solitary mature males.

"A dangerous bear is one that is experiencing stress," Aumiller explains. "Stress may be related to intrusion into the bear's personal space. However, a bear can learn to accept another bear, or a person, into its current personal space without reacting. This is a dynamic process and can change according to the bear's past experiences, as well as other factors like hunger or association with cubs."

"Most information people have about brown bears is not accurate," Stonorov says. "Bears do not have a sinister personality. They are not out to get somebody. They aren't even particularly aggressive. It is difficult for them not to move away from people or other bears. They are always right on the jagged edge of moving off. If we look at them with no preconceived notions, they are not at all a fearsome creature."

Many sanctuary bears display a remarkable tolerance toward humans who are nearby, but others do not. In the early years of the sanctuary, more bears were wary of people than were tolerant. An individual bear that is tolerant toward humans remains so no matter if it is

Left: *These spring cubs seek comfort by being close to one another and to their mother, a small female named Teeny.*
Below: *A mature male pauses from eating a freshly caught salmon to eye photographers on the lower viewing pad at McNeil Falls. Through years of neutral interactions with humans, the bears here go about their daily activities while paying little attention to human onlookers.*

Left: *After a couple of days in the sanctuary, and having seen dozens of bears up close, some visitors shed their fears and become quite relaxed. Here a passing bear glances at the pad and one such visitor. Bears pass close to the viewing pad but are never allowed onto it.* **Below:** *A visitor records the stirrings of Teddy as she awakens from a nap. Teddy regularly feeds, naps, or nurses her cubs in this very spot.*

hungry or even if it has cubs.

"There are many more habituated bears within the sanctuary now than when I first went there," Stonorov notes. "Generation after generation have 'learned' to tolerate or ignore people. They have modified their behavior to treat us neutrally. The most important reason for this is that human behavior has been controlled and become predictable since the early years."

"Bears were, and are, given the option of deciding to be close to us or not," Aumiller explains, "We were in the same place, doing the same things, day in and day out, laying down scent and establishing our predictable patterns. Those that were comfortable came closer, those that were not kept their distance. They practiced avoidance. If they felt comfortable at one hundred or two hundred yards, then fine. We didn't push them. In those days, as now, we thought of the sanctuary as a place for bears, and we did things, as we do now, on a limited basis, giving the bears freedom of movement and access. We inhibit the bears' access when they enter our personal space at only two places, the viewing pad at the falls and the campground. Slowly bears have learned that these sites are off-limits. Over time more bears became tolerant, although there are likely always going to be a number, for a variety of reasons, that don't feel comfortable near people."

This tolerance is the result of both indirect and direct attempts at habituation. Habituation can be described as the process by which a bear becomes accustomed to humans. Aumiller explains that as bears spend time around humans and learn that those interactions are benign they begin to feel comfortable to the extent that they don't purposefully avoid us.

"Larry makes a conscious effort to habituate bears, but not mature males," Stonorov points out. "The process is different for different bears. It is especially important for spring cubs to 'learn' that humans are harmless. The trust grows from there.

"He has a very unique style. He tries to habituate bears in order to create a place where bears and people can co-exist. McNeil River is about the only place in the world where bears can come so close to people with so little risk to either animal."

Some experts believe that habituated bears are very dangerous because usually bears in proximity to humans, such as those in national parks or near public camp-grounds, eventually obtain human food. When a bear makes the connection that people mean food, the odds for continued safe encounters decreases. Food-conditioned bears do not necessarily attack humans for food, but they are around humans, and this proximity promotes trouble.

More than one bear biologist, however, believes that habituation without human food reward may make bears at least in some circumstances less dangerous because it reduces the risk of fear-induced, or stress-induced, aggression. Sanctuary bears are never allowed to obtain human food or garbage and therefore have not associated humans with food.

"It is a generality to say that some bears are tolerant and others are not," Aumiller adds. "Even dealing with bears that are comfortable with people, we still don't surprise them at close quarters. We also make noise in the brush, and don't push them in any way. We still tend to do things safely no matter what bear we're dealing with. A bear, like a dog—any dog and any bear—can be made to bite. It's just a matter of what extreme you must go to before such a response is triggered."

Bears avoid other bears, or humans, because the close proximity of the one to the other builds internal stress. The stress can be relieved either by eliminating exposure to the situation (avoiding the other bear or human) or by increasing tolerance to the situation. Bears tolerate the presence of other bears when tolerance results in a favorable return, such as access to food, that outweighs the associated stress. Research at McNeil shows that as the summer progresses aggression among bears diminishes.

In a situation such as at McNeil River, where bears tolerate one another to an unusual degree, it should not be surprising then to learn that they also tolerate humans.

Cubs learn from their mother, as well as from their own experiences. If the mother is relaxed around people, then the cubs will be relaxed too. Aumiller sees these interactions with females and cubs as of paramount importance. "We want the bears to learn from early on that we are neither a threat nor a source of food or amusement."

"Larry's very careful about not stressing bears," Stonorov observes, "he goes out of his way to avoid doing so. In some instances, he'll make big detours around bears so as not to bother them."

Larry Aumiller photographs a distant bear as a relaxed Teddy stretches out nearby. Photo by Colleen Matt.

Bears fishing for red salmon at the falls on Mikfik Creek in June also attract viewers. Often these are the first people that the bears have encountered since the previous summer's fishing at McNeil Falls. Despite the long lapse in contact, most bears behave just as they do in midsummer in the sanctuary.

Much has been written about a close bear being a dangerous bear. "In surprise encounters, the risk of attack increases in direct relation to the proximity of the bear to the human," reads part of a widely circulated report. From this statement, it is a simple leap of logic that all close contact is hazardous.

Yet, the McNeil experience seems to contradict this view, and Aumiller describes the difference: "There's some confusion about a close bear being a dangerous bear. Proximity to a bear doesn't necessarily mean that it's a dangerous situation. We have several bears that come close, including Teddy who brings her cubs right up to the viewing pad. A large male, named Rusty, had a favorite day bed just twelve feet from the pad. One has to separate out all the variables. If it's an unhabituated bear, one that's not used to being around people, then that can be true. But in our situation where we have a long history with individual, habituated bears, I don't believe that's the case."

Aumiller's comfort with bears at close range didn't develop overnight, nor does he feel comfortable with all bears when in close contact. "Certain individual bears are comfortable very close to humans, and if they are comfortable, so am I. There's been an evolution on their part as well as ours.

"If the bear makes the decision to come close, then chances are they feel unstressed. If they are not stressed, it's a relatively safe situation, despite the fact they're close. Our overriding concern is that the bear makes the decision. That's why we don't just walk right up to one. We try to create a situation where the bears are near us and do it in as safe a way as possible. In a way, we are walking a fine line. While we do things that don't stress bears, or make them wary, at the same time we occasionally have to remind specific bears that people are not something to interact with or be messed with."

It is an evolutionary trait for bears to explore their environment. This exploratory behavior often brings subadults into close proximity to humans. They merely need to check us out, indulge their curiosity, and sometimes see what they can get away with. At McNeil, when a curious subadult gets within a certain distance of the group of people, Aumiller stops its approach with any of a number of escalating responses. Often times a raised hand or a step forward is enough to discourage unwanted close approach. A bear in the campground can be sub-ject to the highest level of negative reinforcement.

"When I first arrived, I felt it necessary to be pretty heavy-handed," Aumiller recalls, "and occasionally used a shotgun with a load of birdshot to drive bears out of camp." Both Faro and Aumiller had to be quite forceful in dealing with bears who had developed habits that made them potentially more dangerous to people. "I bet we used birdshot ten or fifteen times that first year, but over the last six to eight years we've rarely used it, perhaps not at all," Aumiller says. "Cracker shells—noisemakers fired from a shotgun—are used only about two or three times a year now. It's to the point where we can clap our hands and shout and almost every bear has learned to respond by leaving camp."

With negative human-bear interactions almost non-existent in the sanctuary, modern-day visitors see and experience bear behaviors only rarely observed in the late sixties. Many visitors leave the sanctuary not only with good memories of bears but also with an understanding of what has been achieved there.

"I feel that for the last six days I have been 'living with grizzlies,'" visitor Thomas Brown wrote. "Oddly enough it is the *bears* that have allowed me this opportunity to witness their behavior through acceptance and tolerance of humans. The experience has been spiritual in nature and I take with me a greater sense of the importance of protecting wildlife habitat. All legislative decisions affecting this sanctuary should be based solely on what will benefit the bears and not humans."

CONTRARY TO POPULAR MISCONCEPTION, A FEMALE BEAR AT McNeil with spring cubs does not present a terribly difficult or dangerous circumstance. Bears, like Teddy or White, who are tolerant of people, remain tolerant with or without cubs. Spring cubs take their cue from their mother and stay quite close by her. They are fearful of most everything. If the female is calm around humans, they will be too. Within a day or two after arrival, the cubs may even approach humans on their own. Aumiller takes no extraordinary precautions when dealing with them.

Dealing with yearling cubs is another matter. As they gain confidence, yearlings start to venture away from mother a little, but are still dependent on her. "Yearlings are not difficult, but dealing with them and their

After visitors begin to arrive in early June, bears are not allowed in the campground. Because they never get human food or garbage the few young bears that do wander into camp are easy to chase out.

mother as a unit can be complicated," Aumiller admits. "By summer's end the yearling cubs get 'courage,' and being quite curious, they often want to approach people on their own. Depending on the mom, it's a little delicate as to how to discourage those yearlings from coming right up to us. When the cubs get too close, our demeanor switches from essentially neutral to reminding them not to come any closer. But our reminders have to be done so that the mom's happy with what we're doing, too. Even though she's tolerant of humans, she wouldn't allow us to harm her cubs. We're not only responding in a way that's going to impact the cubs but her as well. Hopefully we do something that isn't going to distress her but will stop the cubs' progress toward us."

During their third summer, these same cubs are then on their own and have lost "status" by not having their mother to protect them any more. "They've gone down in dominance and can be quite easily made to stay away from people. There's a whole series of things that can be done to discourage unwanted behavior in adolescent bears," Aumiller explains. "The simplest is just to look at

them, and in some situations that's enough. I've actually turned my back on a young bear to show disregard, a sign of stature among bears. That was enough. In general, bears do seem to read human body language.

"These two-and-a-half-year-olds are sometimes curious and will approach. They're on their own. They've been around people for a couple of years, but they're a little bit insecure, and you can make them run away at full speed if that's your intent. Move toward them, make noise, and as a last resort, charge them.

"The next year they're three-and-a-half-year-olds, they've been on their own for a year, and they're starting to get a little bit bolder. They're comfortable around humans because we've been predictable and proved that we're harmless. They do have a natural curiosity, and I'm sure given the opportunity, most tolerant bears at McNeil River would want to put their noses on people and get a good sniff in order to see what we are about.

"So we must decide at what point we don't want them any closer and respond in a way that discourages them. The key is not to overdo it. I don't want the bear

Immature bears spend a good deal of their time futilely chasing salmon in the shallow waters of Mikfik Creek. These energetic pursuits often amuse viewers.

to avoid us completely or never come by camp again because of a negative encounter. It's a fine line to dissuade them, get them to ignore us, without making them totally avoid us in the future.

"Close approach and aggression, these are the two things we want to modify. I firmly believe that bears can learn in just one encounter a behavior that is unacceptable. They learn fast."

Just holding ground—the group of people not retreating—is sometimes enough to stop a bear from approaching. "Say a two-year-old is pressing in on us," Aumiller hypothesized. "If he could get us to retreat a step he'd find that encouraging, and so he might press in a little more. But by virtue of just holding our ground, ignoring him, we are making a statement. A very low-key one, but that's maybe all it takes."

Bears, like any animal, travel through life and either receive reward or punishment for each behavior. Some actions bring what are called neutral rewards: Nothing good, nothing bad happens. Behaviors that result in something negative occurring are readily abandoned. Other behaviors that end in a food reward may carry a bit of "punishment" with them. An example is a bear who, in the process of stealing a fish from another bear, ends up being bitten but gets away with the fish anyway. These behaviors persist despite the cost.

"If a behavior is food related, the dynamics change," Aumiller explains. "A bear is much more willing to take punishment if in the end it gets the reward of food. If curiosity is the sole motivation, a bear is less likely to tolerate being hassled and is more easily discouraged."

Here Aumiller is referring to encounters with very young bears, where all the bear is really doing is attempting to satisfy its curiosity. And it doesn't take much to restore the balance. "To them the situation is not vital; they see that things are not working out because the group appears unimpressed or unintimidated and, well fine, they turn about and go on with other things."

People management is the critical factor. Maintaining a group size of up to ten is an important point because bears behave differently when people are alone or in small groups. In terms of safety, a group of five to ten is safer than a group of fewer than three to five.

"At McNeil I never think in terms of 'me,'" Aumiller adds, "I think in terms of the group demeanor and presence. This is critical. I sometimes direct the group to spread out, which makes us look more impressive, or to huddle together, which reduces the bears' stress level or encourages them to come closer."

Group size is important, not only to ensure safety, but to limit adverse impact on the bears. Small groups are easier to control and maneuver in response to the bears. Group behavior is more consistent and predictable. People have a whole variety of responses to bears: get closer, run away screaming, crawl up to a sleeping bear in the grass—almost anything. But with the elimination of negative and bizarre human behaviors, bears gradually become more tolerant of people.

"Perhaps we overdo it and pussyfoot around more than we really need to," Aumiller admits, "but in a managed system where we have the ability to do that, and there's no negative reason not to, then we might as well go that last step and be as safe as we can. In all the decisions we make day to day, if we always work with safety as our bottom line, we then tend to make proper and consistent decisions."

"UNPREDICTABLE"—THE MOST COMMON ADJECTIVE USED TO describe bears. "The term usually implies that bears have the capacity to attack people," Stonorov observes, "but it is a grossly inaccurate term. Ninety-nine point nine percent of what happens at McNeil, and elsewhere for that matter, is predictable."

"It's a poor term not only because bears are predictable but because it implies that bears have a whole range of options the same as people," Aumiller adds. "They really only have two when they're stressed: flee or fight. By always using this term 'unpredictable,' people seem to think that they are at the whim of chance and that ultimately it doesn't matter what they do around bears. Their reasoning takes the turn that it doesn't really matter if they keep a clean camp, or make noise on the trail, or dispose of garbage properly, because no matter what they do, something bad could easily happen because of the bears' 'unpredictability.'"

"Bears seem unpredictable because our knowledge of an individual bear's behavior is incomplete," Faro adds. "Bears do not hold 'grudges,' the old 'killer-bear' syndrome. This view is an anthropomorphic one that holds that bears should behave in such a manner because we would. It doesn't work like that. The term 'unpredict-

Above: *Many female brown bears well past twenty years of age will still have cubs. Red Collar was twenty-four when this cub, her last, was born.* **Right:** *The first chum salmon arrive at McNeil River usually on the day the first wild irises bloom. This bear hasn't long to wait for a meal of fresh fish.*

able' only means our knowledge is incomplete.

"Aumiller, for example, more than anyone else in the world, has the biggest backlog of information on what bears will do, and that's why he can read them so well."

According to researchers, confrontations between grizzly bears and people in national parks have historically fallen into three broad categories: unexpected close-range encounters in areas where visibility is reduced; "crowding" by photographers, campers, or hikers; and aggressive foraging in campgrounds by bears that have learned to associate human presence with food. The latter scenario has proven the most likely of the three to result in human fatality.

From these scenarios, it would be easy to develop a simple set of rules that would prevent most bear-human confrontations: make noise while hiking, avoid dense brush, never run from a bear, keep human food and garbage away from bears, avoid approaching bears, especially females with young. Most of these rules have been publicized by various agencies that manage public lands.

In the sanctuary, because bears are accustomed to seeing and being around people, they have lost much of their innate fear of us. Yet these simple rules of conduct are as rigorously applied in the sanctuary as they would be applied elsewhere by prudent people. Unfortunately, throughout most of the world's diminishing brown bear habitat humans are often unwilling to follow even these few simple guidelines.

As the McNeil experience indicates, bears do have a fairly predictable set of responses to most situations. Some of the well-known bears exhibit no special interest in humans.

"We don't offer food, threat, or competition. We might as well be rocks, for all that these bears are concerned," Aumiller points out. "But they are not harmless."

Every effort is made to ensure safety, but any outdoor activity is never completely without risks. Faro predicts, "One day someone will be hurt by a bear in the sanctuary. It will happen in an incidental encounter, a bear escaping from another bear, or a similar circumstance where a person just happens to be in the way or in the wrong place at the wrong time. This should be an assumable risk, however, part of visiting the sanctuary, and nothing extraordinary made of it. It will happen."

"Bears are large powerful animals with plenty of

equipment to do us bodily harm should they so desire," Aumiller explains. "Hence we should respect them. But not having absolute control over large animals does not mean we can't coexist with them. Native people did, long before effective weapons were invented. You can bet they respected bears."

Therein lies the key: respect.

The close proximity of other bears is stressful for young cubs. Spring cubs that are left alone when their mother goes fishing often crowd together for reassurance.

A BEAR NAMED WHITE

LATE ONE JUNE EVENING IN 1985, LARRY Aumiller was in camp working alone on a maintenance project when his colleague, biologist Polly Hessing, rushed in with the news that the year's first female with cubs had appeared on the gravel spit. Up until then, just a few bears had been seen in the sanctuary.

"Each year, it is exciting to see the first cubs," Aumiller recalls. "Part of it involves trying to identify individual bears we've gotten to know over time and to see which ones make it back. Spring cubs are always of special interest, not just because of who their mother might be, but because we always try to approach the families more carefully, give them more room, and in general behave more cautiously. It is very important to know which females have spring cubs so that when visitors are in camp, we will know which bears to approach or to avoid.

"We crept out there and stood on the beach in front of the cabin. The bear was on top of the spit just two hundred yards from camp, and since she was partially hidden by driftwood, we couldn't identify her. It was dusk, and raining, and visibility wasn't all that great. All we could do was wait for the bear to move into the open.

"We waited quite awhile and couldn't tell if the bear had noticed us or not, so we decided to move to a closer vantage point. By the time we reached higher ground, the bear had actually bedded down. We soon saw that she had at least one spring cub. Nestled in among the driftwood logs as they were, we still couldn't get an identification. I was growing a bit apprehensive about going closer, so I made a little noise to alert the bear of our presence. The bear hardly reacted. Now I was more puzzled than apprehensive but decided not to go any closer. Night was quickly coming on. I had just determined to head back to the cabin when suddenly the bear got to her feet and faced our direction. At this point, we were two hundred feet from her. She still showed no unusual reaction. The cubs, who were five or ten feet from their mother,

Left: *Taken in the mid-1980s, this portrait of White depicts her in the prime of life. Her new fall coat is beginning to grow in and she's waddling fat from a summer's diet of fish.* **Inset:** *Two spring cubs crowd in close to White.*

A Chronology of White's Life

Year	Age	Activity
1969	0.5	With two siblings as spring cubs
1970	1.5	Alone
1971	2.5	Immobilized by biologist first time
1972	3.5	Immobilized second time, almost drowned
1973	4.5	Alone
1974	5.5	Alone
1975	6.5	In estrus for first time
1976	7.5	With first litter of two cubs
1977	8.5	With only one yearling
1978	9.5	Alone and mating with Harpo
1979	10.5	With three spring cubs, lost one during summer
1980	11.5	With two yearlings
1981	12.5	With two two-and-one-half-year-old offspring
1982	13.5	Alone
1983	14.5	Alone
1984	15.5	With three spring cubs
1985	16.5	With three yearlings, one killed in July by another bear after getting separated from family
1986	17.5	With two two-and-one-half-year-old offspring
1987	18.5	Alone
1988	19.5	Alone but with wound on neck, had lost much weight
1989	20.5	Alone and mating with Waldo and LDMF
1990	21.5	With three spring cubs, lost one in unknown circumstance
1991	22.5	With two yearlings

Left: *White finishes off a salmon on the bluff above McNeil Falls while a cacophonous swirl of gulls awaits scraps. White favors the side of the river near the viewing pad, an area most dominant males avoid because of people.*
Above: *Often White and her cubs appear in the sanctuary in early spring before the arrival of most other bears. Her long-time use of the sanctuary, coupled with a remarkable tolerance for people, has allowed people the opportunity to learn a great deal about bears.*

saw us, stood up on their hind legs, then dropped down, and ran to mom.

"They scooted underneath her, as cubs do for protection, but her behavior still did not change. Then she started walking slowly in our direction, the cubs pushing in tight against her. We then were faced with the dilemma of wanting to get out of her way, while also wanting to move into the open where we could be seen clearly. Since it was imperative that she see us, we actually moved down onto the open mudflats. The bears kept coming towards us.

"Within moments, it was obvious that the bear was White. We just stood our ground and watched her walk on by, the cubs tucked in tight to her flank. The cubs were concerned and kept looking at us, but all White did was glance at us briefly and keep going. She passed within twenty yards of us.

"Seeing these favorite bears show up, especially with spring cubs, is always exciting and special. We hadn't seen White in maybe eight or nine months, and just to know that she had survived late autumn, winter, and early spring was really gratifying.

"We'd come out for what I thought would be only a few moments, but we stayed thirty minutes. We were so enthralled with what transpired that we pretty much ignored the rain. Suddenly I realized that we were without raingear and were completely soaked to the bone. But I didn't care, my joy was enveloping. White was back."

EXCEPT FOR THE FACT THAT WHITE IS ONE OF A HANDFUL OF bears that have lived long and full lives in the vicinity of humans, she is much like other female brown bears. Her experiences offer insight into the life of an individual bear and its interactions with both humans and bears at McNeil River, as well as being representative in some measure of her species.

She was born in late 1968 or early 1969, and was one of a trio of cubs that in 1970 became known by biologists as "The Three Bears." These female siblings were remarkable for their similar size and shape and beautiful blonde coats. They traveled about the sanctuary together and, as a result, enjoyed a higher social rank among bears than they would have had individually. Though somewhat nervous around the bigger bears, the trio did fish at the falls, with White being the most aggressive and adept at catching fish.

The identity of the mother of the Three Bears is not known for certain, but Derek Stonorov, an early researcher at the sanctuary, believes she was a bear named O.D.—or Olive Drab, the color of her collar—who was born in 1960, and tagged in 1963. Jim Faro removed her collar in 1972.

"We do not know White's lineage," Faro counters, disagreeing with Stonorov. "She showed up in 1970, with her sisters and without their mother. O.D. had just two spring cubs in 1969."

In Aumiller's opinion, "the behavior of White and her sisters, and their tolerance toward people, points to the fact that they likely were the offspring of a McNeil 'regular,' like O.D., or another tolerant female."

As part of the brown bear life-history research program then in progress in the sanctuary, the Three Bears were each immobilized with a drug fired from a dart gun and given red, white, and blue ear tags. Their ear-tag colors provided their names.

One evening in July 1971, Faro darted White on the tidal flats, and within eight minutes she was immobilized. At the time of capture, she was traveling with her two siblings who ran off. Measurements were taken, eartags affixed to each ear, a number tattooed inside her lip, and a tooth pulled to determine her exact age. She is officially known by her ear-tag number as bear #39. Faro estimated her weight at two hundred pounds and her age at three and a half. (Just as a tree can be aged by counting its rings, an animal can be aged by examining the cementum layers in a tooth. Based on tooth analysis, White was two and a half when tagged.) A few days later, White, with ear tags in place, was again seen with her siblings.

Sometime after leaving the sanctuary that fall, possibly about denning time, or perhaps even the following spring, White broke contact with her siblings. Red and Blue continued as a unit in 1972 and were together again for part of the summer of 1973. White, who had displayed her independence in 1971 by aggressive fishing at the falls, was on her own.

On July 27, 1972, White was again immobilized by Faro. The first dart failed to fire. The second worked, and the drug took effect within three minutes. She was darted while walking in the intertidal area behind the spit. Her

In 1990, White nurses her two spring cubs in the grass above the viewing pad. This bear's behavior toward people is little changed by the presence of cubs. With or without young she remains tolerant and non-aggressive toward people.

weight was estimated at two hundred fifty pounds. Her lip-tattoo was redone. After completing their work, the tagging crew moved White, still under the effects of the drug, to the base of the spit to avoid leaving her exposed to the incoming tide. After returning to camp for lunch, Faro was unavoidably delayed and unable to return to White as soon as he had planned. He became quite concerned when he noticed the flood tide. He calculated the length of time needed for the drug to wear off. His calculations only increased his apprehension.

Faro rushed back and from the gravel spit saw White floating in the water, two-thirds submerged. Her head was underwater, and bubbles were coming up. Faro raced to White and dragged her out of the water and onto shore where he began pushing on her side. Water flowed from her mouth and nose. He rolled her over and repeated the process with the same result. Finally she began to revive. Faro backed off. In a short while, White got to her feet and stumbled toward the driftwood on the top of the spit. Faro breathed a big sigh of relief, happy that the unavoidable delay had not resulted in tragedy. It was at least twenty-four hours, Faro said, before White's normal and complete vigor seemed restored. She was seen grazing on the flats three days later.

"It was purely a case of human error," Faro admits, "and we were within ten to thirty seconds of losing her. Later, despite all the handling and the near disaster, she displayed absolutely no increased aversion to people, or fear. She was the same old White."

White's early behavior around humans set her apart. She approached people, especially lone individuals, and pressed in on them, making her "victims" uncomfortable. She sometimes approached from a long way off and was hard to deter. Because she also spent a lot of time near camp, she was often in camp and consequently around people. Utah State University graduate student Tom Bledsoe worked at McNeil River from 1973 to 1975, and had some intense moments with White. Several times White got on his trail and followed him.

"Tom was good around bears, he knew what to do, he didn't panic or run," Aumiller recalls. "He kept up a steady pace, and if she got too close, he would stop and she would stop too. He walked, she walked. He stopped, she stopped. That sort of thing. Once when this was going on, he got out of sight and ran until he was far enough away that when she came into view, the attraction was broken. I remember, once in 1976, watching her follow him across the flats at a slow, steady pace, never varying the distance."

Jim Faro adds that researcher Allen Egbert also had problems with White. According to Faro, she seemed to single Egbert out. She bluff-charged him several times. Faro thinks she was trying to get him to run. She followed him as she did author Tom Bledsoe. Faro surmises part of the problem was that the researchers worked alone a lot of the time, unlike visitors who traveled in groups. Aumiller doubts that White singled out specific people; more likely she singled out any lone individuals.

Aumiller actually remembers White following him a couple of times during his first season. "It was somewhat nerve-wracking because of all that misinformation that we've all been exposed to," he said. "Most of it suggests that bears have only one kind of demeanor toward people, and that's aggression, and for a bear to show any interest, whatsoever, even at a distance, a person should be nervous. Today I can only speculate that because of her youth, she felt the need to test people a bit. Young bears do it to one another all the time. It's a normal process for a young bear. We can't really know her motivations. Maybe there's some sort of low-level positive feedback for doing those things, like dominance building. Perhaps if a person turned and walked away at precisely the right moment, it would fulfill some subtle need for the bear to take advantage of that little chink in the human armor. In the last ten years, I can't remember another bear that did this nearly as much as White, although various youngsters have tried it a time or two."

Because White was unintimidated by people, and often grazed near camp, perhaps it was inevitable, given the haphazard camp conditions in those years, that White would run afoul of people. Carelessness with human food encouraged White to become what Faro called a "camp terror."

"This year for the first time since I've been there, we had bear problems at McNeil," Faro wrote after the 1972 field season. "Two groups of photographers did not heed advice about food storage and suffered property losses. In an attempt to establish a little bit of property rights, I was forced to turn a 20-gauge shotgun and fire birdshot on a bear [White] in the sanctuary."

After the incidents with the photographers' food boxes, one of which was filled with sausage and salamis, White became very hard to deter. Altogether, White was birdshot in camp five or six times in 1972. She came into

Even with cubs, White spends considerable time fishing McNeil Falls. Here she shares a fish-filled riffle with an adult male, all the while keeping herself between him and her two-and-a-half-year-old cubs.

camp and destroyed tents. After the fourth tent was destroyed, Faro birdshot her, at a distance of about fifty to sixty feet, and her hindquarters slumped to the ground. Obviously she was injured beyond what was intended. She regained her feet and ran out of camp, across Mikfik Flats, and up into the brush on the bluffs. She lay there for three or four days. Faro, quite concerned, checked on her each day. He thought that she might die—and all as a result of people's carelessness with food storage. On the fifth day, he decided that if she hadn't improved, he would kill her rather than let her suffering continue. It seemed the humane thing to do. To his relief, he found her grazing on the flats in an apparently normal fashion. She seemed fully recovered.

Generally a very lightweight load of birdshot fired at a distance does not wound a bear but delivers a powerful "sting." Today rubber bullets or rubber shot are sometimes used. These projectiles are not completely riskfree, but they are generally much less injurious than misplaced shot.

"She was coming into camp at night, getting into occupied tents. It was an escalating situation, with someone likely to get hurt. Shooting her with birdshot was a strategy designed to give her one last chance before we resorted to destroying her," Faro explains, "We were trying to undo all the bad habits she'd picked up in the past. I admit it was drastic action, but it worked. Later, when she walked into camp, all I had to do was work the action on the shotgun and upon hearing this she would turn around and walk out of camp. She had 'learned.' Again, as following the near-drowning, she was still the same bear; her behavior, other than foraging in camp, did not change."

White has turned into one of the most tolerant bears. Because of her long record of nonaggressive behavior and indifference to humans, White may be one of the safest McNeil bears to be around. She long ago stopped following people. Now she displays essentially no interest in people at all. Faro attributes the change to maturation; her earlier negative behavior that went unrewarded has been discarded. In fact, by 1977, her demeanor had undergone what Tom Bledsoe, the graduate student young

Above: *Salmon that have spawned and died or that have been killed by other bears wash downstream and are salvaged by bears. White searches the shallow water for scraps and carcasses.* **Inset:** *Mating season peaks in May but lasts into June or, rarely, July. Tim mates with White at McNeil Falls.*

White had pursued, described as a "remarkable metamorphosis." The previous year, she had her first litter of cubs, and one of them accompanied her throughout the 1977 season. Despite being accompanied by a cub and despite the trauma of losing another cub, both mythical reasons often claimed to make a bear more dangerous, White had mellowed.

White's first estrus was recorded in 1975, and she had her first two cubs the next year, at age seven and a half. Her sister Blue had her first cub in 1978 at age nine and a half. Blue was not seen again after the summer of 1978. Red, the third sibling, had her first litter in 1975, at age six and a half. (At McNeil, the mean age at first litter is six and a half.) Red also was extremely tolerant even when accompanied by cubs. She provided numerous close observations and photographic opportunities in 1975. Pictures of her and her cubs graced the pages of innumerable books, calendars, and magazines. Unfortunately she met an early death. She was killed in the fall of 1975, in "defense of life and property," at the mouth of the Gibraltar River. Faro remembers that her cubs were also shot and killed in the same incident. Often when bears are seen at close range or approaching, people become fearful and presume they are being "attacked." Bears drawn by scent into fish camps are also perceived as threatening.

White has been a very fertile and productive female. She has not missed many years when she could produce young and has been very successful in raising at least part of each litter. She was seen in early July 1978, breeding with four different males. The following spring, she arrived with three cubs. Since 1976, and through 1991, she has produced eleven cubs, seven of which lived at least until the end of the second summer.

Aumiller cautions that since very few sanctuary bears are marked, positive identification of young bears is tentative. Because of year-to-year photographic records, natural scars and marks, and behavior, he is confident of most adult identifications.

Because two-year-old cubs, once they leave their mother, are hard to recognize individually, it's difficult to track White's cubs into their third summer. As a result, their fate is often unknown. Biologist Polly Hessing however, documented a dramatic end to one of White's cubs.

On June 16, 1985, White, then sixteen, showed up on the Mikfik Flats with three yearling cubs. They grazed in the sedge flats and fished for red salmon in Mikfik

Creek. About July 8, one of the cubs, W.C. (White's Cub), became separated from the family group. White and her two remaining cubs moved to McNeil River while W.C. continued to graze on the flats. Being very young, this bear exhibited considerable nervousness and avoided other bears, thereby inhibiting his chances of reconnecting with his family then fishing at McNeil Falls. A new female with two spring cubs, one dark-furred and one light-furred, arrived on the flats on July 16. W.C. spent much of the next two days within about one hundred yards of this family group. Observers said that he seemed to want to join the family, which is not unusual behavior for newly weaned bears. The new female tolerated W.C.'s presence to within ten feet of her.

The next day, Hessing witnessed W.C.'s unexpected and violent death. "The female bear stood at the water's edge, with one of her cubs 25 feet . . . behind her," Hessing wrote. "Then I noticed two more [young] bears coming over the spit walking side by side towards the female, one was [her] lighter-colored cub and the other W.C. The [female's dark] cub [approached to] within five feet . . . of the pair, then they all turned and approached the female. The dark-colored cub ran to the female and they touched noses. W.C. stopped briefly when about 15 feet . . . from the female who had been facing away out into the lagoon. She turned as W.C. came to within three feet. . . . The female swung her head sideways and lashed out with a foreleg. W.C. whirled and ran. He didn't get far. He slipped and was caught from behind after only making 20 feet. . . . The female grabbed W.C. by the neck and threw him down. He tried to rise but each time she flung him down again. She did not let up. Her cubs watched from 30 feet away and uttered loud cries.

"The female bit his head several times and grabbed his neck and shook him. I could see her tearing at his leg. I could see flesh and bone. I thought W.C. was dead, but I saw him raise his head and try to get up. The female bit his skull several more times before again grabbing him by the neck."

Within about four or five minutes, W.C. was dead and the female was feeding upon his carcass. Only a tiny proportion, perhaps 10 percent, of the 140-pound yearling was consumed. The attack was not motivated by hunger. W.C.'s close approach perhaps triggered the attack, which then turned fatal when he slipped and fell and was set upon. Unable to get away, or exhibit submis-

sive body posture, W.C.'s fate was sealed. The female was thereafter known as Idi—Idi Amin.

Another kind of tale can be told about White and her cubs of another year. She produced three cubs in 1990, but one was "lost" over the winter through unknown circumstances. Her two remaining cubs were of contrasting color, one light and the other dark. The light one almost always nursed on White's right side, the dark one on her left. Twenty-one out of twenty-four times, they were on their favored sides. The arrangement was the source of many human wagers throughout the summer.

Earlier in the summer, this bear family also delighted visitors. White and her two yearling cubs were seen feeding behind camp one day. Within a short while, one of the visitors came running up to tell Aumiller that White and her cubs were in the pond by the sauna. "You've got to see this," the woman said.

"I ran down there, and sure enough, the bears were in the pond," Aumiller remembers. "White wasn't in long but the cubs played with the lily flowers and pads for quite some time. They'd submerge under the pads and surface with them draped over their faces. They seemed to enjoy running the pads over their heads. They batted the pads and flowers back and forth. To see this tolerant female and her cubs wading and playing among the yellow flowers and lily pads by the sauna was quite pleasing."

Because of her ear-tags, which offer positive identification, White holds the longevity record for sanctuary "regulars." Lanky is probably older than White, and may hold the record for productivity. She once was tagged and has a lip tattoo, but that is not readable unless she's immobilized, so her productivity and longevity records at this point are not so easily documented. Lanky had a single cub in 1991 at an estimated age of twenty-six. Wild, free-roaming brown bears may live to thirty years, although twenty years is the usual top end of their life span. The oldest bear of any species was a captive female brown bear who was euthanized at forty-five. She had her last litter at forty-two.

WHERE WHITE GOES WHEN SHE LEAVES THE SANCTUARY IS MERE conjecture.

"We don't really know where White spends her time when not in the sanctuary. In May 1985, I saw her on

Trailed by her cubs, White passes close to viewers stationed on the lower viewing pad at McNeil Falls. Having learned from their mother that humans are non-threatening, neutral entities in the sanctuary, White's adult offspring—and their cubs—display similar behavior toward people and form the core group of the sanctuary's super-tolerant bears.

Paint River," Aumiller recalls. "I didn't recognize her right away. I was walking up the river and came around some brush, and there was a bear walking straight at me. We saw each other at the same time; I stopped, but it kept coming. I didn't have a gun or much time to react because it was quite close. I thought about jumping in the river but instead just backed up a few feet into the brush. The bear walked by within fifteen feet and continued on to the intertidal area. It seemed so nonchalant that I was sure it was a McNeil bear. I followed it at a distance and soon recognized her as White."

Not only does Aumiller's observation reveal one animal's movement outside the sanctuary to the north, it also demonstrates that a tolerant bear may react to people in a neutral fashion in areas away from the sanctuary. In contrast, Jim Faro once encountered a known bear, Flower Child, on Pinkadulia Creek south of McNeil. Flower Child got her name because she retained the red ear-flagging placed on her in 1968, which gave her the appearance of wearing a flower behind her ear. Outside the sanctuary, and in a place where it did not regularly encounter people, this normally tolerant bear panicked when it saw Faro, and ran off. He suggests behaviors in and out

of the sanctuary may vary and be more complex than we know.

McNeil bears likely disperse to all points of the compass. Just because she was seen on the Paint River, and her sister Red was shot to the north on Gibraltar River, it can't be assumed that White and her siblings always went north. In fact, because the area to the north is open to hunting, it can be argued that there is a selection process that favors bears that go south or southwest, areas now closed to hunting. Because she has been around a long time, and often is the first bear to show up in the spring, usually late May, and the last to leave in the fall, about mid-September, Aumiller surmises that White cannot be going far.

Movements and home ranges of all sanctuary bears are largely unknown. "We don't know much about movements," Aumiller says. "It would be doubtful if many bears stay the whole year in the sanctuary. Because of its size—it is essentially just a drainage, with long, thin proportions—I doubt if any bears live their whole lives within it. Rather, the sanctuary is part of overlapping home ranges. For some bears, McNeil River might be the southern edge of their home range, for others it might be the northern extreme. If any bear stays the entire year in the sanctuary, or at least spends the majority of its annual cycle within it, chances are the bear is a female because females have smaller home ranges than do males."

Because of the way she uses the sanctuary, White quite likely dens nearby. There is still snow on the ground when she emerges from hibernation, and food is scarce. She will eat anything she can find. Bears elsewhere along the coast regularly dig clams, but Kamishak Bay is poor for clams. However, Faro has watched White dig soft-shelled clams on the McNeil Cove tidal flats.

White returned to the sanctuary in the spring of 1988 with one of the most hideous wounds ever seen on a bear there. Scars and wounds on males from dominance battles are not uncommon, but this was something else. She showed up with a huge open wound on the right side of her neck. She was so thin, down from her adult weight of 450 pounds, that she was not initially recognizable. Aumiller remembers, "We at first called her Hamburger Neck. We watched her for days, thinking she was a young, submissive female. But she was doing the same sort of things White would do, like ambling down the path past the viewing pad at the falls and down the stairs to the river. Then one day at the falls, we glimpsed a bit of broken ear-tag. Because her appearance had changed so much, we weren't sure until then. The wound was a ghastly sight, twelve inches across and somewhat convex. Perhaps it was the result of infection; it seemed to grow. A visiting physician speculated that it was a carcinoma. It did finally heal so that wasn't right. We've never seen anything like it at McNeil."

The year 1991 was White's twenty-second year at the sanctuary. Throughout the summer Aumiller remarked to visitors on her importance. Especially during his early years in the sanctuary, White was one of the bears instrumental in "teaching" him about bears and the human response to them.

"From the very start, Faro was insistent that I was in charge and supposed to run things. He was there four or five days and then he would leave. Although I'd been around bears some, this was different. These were tolerant bears, and they behaved unlike any bears that I'd been around. All of the things that I usually experienced—like the bears running away—didn't happen," he recalls.

"It was mostly on-the-job training. Armed with a rifle, off I'd go. I was so unsure at times, my heart rate

must have been 190. That first year was very tentative. I often overreacted and usually at great distances. A group of visitors and I would spend half an hour at three hundred yards from a bear, half an hour at two hundred yards, half an hour at one hundred yards, and so on, before moving closer. We didn't purposefully get real close. But I soon learned that with White you didn't need to be standoffish. Often she ended up moving towards us, but not aggressively. She just seemed to feel unthreatened and continued to graze or catch fish nearby. When she'd get close, we'd just stand our ground. That was Faro's main instruction, let things happen around us. And they did. She was often our satellite."

White accelerated the pace of learning about bears because of the situations that developed around her, Aumiller remembers. By moving in, instead of away, she offered the chance for people to spend long periods of time with her and learn more about cubs, or to observe even the wary, amorous mature males that were lured in close to her during her estrus period.

She has mated with some large males—Chaser, Waldo, Romeo, and others—some of which were not especially tolerant of people. Chaser was typical. He would follow her in close to people but exhibit stress behavior. However, over the years, this "forced" proximity led Chaser through an accelerated habituation process, and he became less wary than some in his older male cohort.

White also was one of the first bears who began to nurse her cubs near people. In the early years, people rarely saw bears nursing, even at a distance. Bears seem to need a secure, comfortable situation in which to nurse their cubs. Faro remembers a female or two in 1975 who would nurse cubs or leave cubs near humans, but White offered the first regular opportunity to get good close observations of this behavior. It was then that observers heard the vocalizations that accompany nursing: the cubs emit an almost catlike purring. Later, it was White's adult offspring Teddy who brought her cubs in even closer to people.

In spring 1991, Teddy was being pursued across Mikfik Flats by a large male. Aumiller was with a group of visitors stationed along the lower part of the creek when Teddy came by. "The big male was uncomfortable being that close to us, and hung back. Teddy made a tight circle around us, and in an effort to keep up with her, the male made a bigger circle around that. She circled three times. He was forced each time to cover an immense amount of ground just to keep pace. He did that until the fourth circle when she got a little ahead. That put us between her and the male. This seemed to make him even more uncomfortable, and he broke off and went away. Almost at once she lay down and went to sleep right next to us." Aumiller cautions against assuming that a cognitive process was at work whereby Teddy thought out the effect of the humans on the male and used the people to ward him off.

In spite of himself, Aumiller has felt a growing attachment to White. "You try not to have favorites," he explains, "and I tried not to . . . and strive not to. It tends to cloud your objectivity. But, in fact, you do have favorites. White's been around a long time, she's been available, and, let's face it, if you like animals, it's hard not to like a furry critter you've spent lots of time around."

Even veteran biologists are sometimes affected by their experiences at the sanctuary. Wildlife management biologists, when proposing hunting seasons and bag limits, tend not to think of individual animals but rather in terms of animal populations.

"Ten years ago I seldom thought of individuals," Dick Sellers recalled in 1991. "I thought only of managing populations. I remember the sanctuary staff and some visitors being upset that Zubin, an old favorite, had been killed by a hunter the year before. It meant nothing to me. Although we can't manage for individual animals, and I must still manage for populations, I now have a tremendous interest in certain individual bears. It would trouble me to learn that White or Teddy had died, no matter the cause."

A bear that makes itself visible on a regular basis is bound to draw special attention. Where White fished, and to a degree how she fished, was a result of several factors, as is true with all bears at McNeil Falls. Each has a preference for certain spots under certain conditions. Water level, presence of other bears, proximity to humans, and past experience both as cubs and adults, all play a part. White, in part because she is tolerant of people, almost always fishes the south side of the falls near the viewing pad. She mostly fishes the upper falls, but on occasion she will move to the lower falls. She seldom goes to the north side of the river, so consequently she is generally close to visitors at the pad. White is one of the few bears who will actually walk the boardwalk to the pad. She regularly passes close to people on the pad before descending the stairs to the falls. "She's

tended to come closer and closer to the pad," Aumiller observes, "coming so close, in fact, if you tried, you could lean out and touch her."

Importantly, as a result of White's tolerance, now six or seven bears exhibit similar behavior, most of them her offspring. Teddy, her adult female offspring, who was born in 1979, is the next generation that displays this remarkable tolerance for humans. "Teddy is even more tolerant than White," Derek Stonorov points out. "She'll actually nurse her cubs near the pad and spend time around us."

"Seeing that mama bear nurse her cubs right next to us was the most exciting and memorable experience of my life as a photographer," Helen Rhode reveals. Her picture of the nursing family was seen in the February 1986 *National Geographic* magazine article on grizzlies.

Michio Hoshino, a photographer who's been lucky enough to visit the sanctuary on ten occasions, remembers one truly magic moment between bears and humans. "One day Colleen Matt, Larry Aumiller, and I were sitting on the river bank, watching Teddy and her two spring cubs fishing for salmon. They had moved very close to us. All at once, Teddy started coming right toward us. Larry cautioned me not to move, but it was hard, very hard not to want to leave. She came right up on the bank next to us and sat down. The cubs were nervous and excited, but Teddy completely ignored us. Eventually the cubs quieted down. Soon, I relaxed, too. I wish I could have taken a picture of that scene. Three people sitting side by side on a riverbank with three bears."

Teddy produced her first cub, a male, named Ted, in 1985. He's seven years old now and displays this same astounding tolerance for humans. Just like Teddy and White, he walks the boardwalk to the pad, then descends the stairs to the river. If he survives the conflicts of male adulthood, his development in behavior toward people as he bulks up will be quite interesting.

In 1991, Teddy's new two-and-a-half-year-old cubs, Willie and Khutzy, were on their own and displaying the same tolerance noted during their first year of life. "One day at the falls in 1991, my attention was on other bears, when I suddenly had this feeling that there was something next to me," Aumiller remembers. "I looked up and there were Willie and Khutzy sitting three to four feet away, just looking at the river. They were in the same spot where White or Teddy always spend time, a place where virtually no other bears go because it's so close to people. They appeared nervous about being around other bears and didn't stay very long. The mere fact that they chose to sit right next to us, however, makes me think that those two females will behave exactly as has their mother, Teddy, and their grandmother, White."

Above: One of White's yearling cubs takes an exploratory swim in the pond near the campground sauna. Because White is comfortable near people, her cubs learn the same. **Right:** All bears, especially females with cubs, keep a close watch on nearby bears. White and her two yearlings closely watch another bear fishing below them in Mikfik Creek. **Overleaf:** Spring cubs take their behavioral cues from their mother. Here White's spring cub joins her in a meal of tough sedge grass.

AMID THE GATHERING

SIXTY-SEVEN BROWN BEARS HAVE BEEN seen at one time in the one-half mile of river adjacent to McNeil Falls. This congregation of brown bears is both unparalleled and highly unusual for this species that typically is asocial.

Mature brown bears are solitary, with a simple social system. Affiliations between bears are limited to family groups—a female and her cubs—and to litter mates that remain together for up to three years after separation from their mother. Male-female consorts form for brief periods during the spring mating season. Other temporary affiliations, such as play bouts, also form on occasion. These are the exceptions to the solitary life of a brown bear.

Loose congregations, like those at McNeil River, are transient. In these situations, some of the same social behaviors associated with gregarious species appear. As the salmon run builds and bears congregate to take advantage of it, a social hierarchy develops. Low-intensity ritualized behavior displays replace more potentially damaging behaviors, thus minimizing risk of injury to adults and death of subadults.

Animal social structure has developed in response to competition for food, mates, and denning or nesting sites. The most complex social orders appear in species that cooperate in the hunt or that live in troops or packs like baboons and wolves. Animals that defend individual exclusive territories also have fairly complex social structures.

Bears, however, do not defend exclusive territories but live in home ranges that overlap with other bears. "A home range is essentially that area in which a bear lives and is likely to be found," biologist Derek Stonorov explains. "Within it are all of its life requirements—food, shelter, mates, and denning areas."

A home range can either be seasonal, perennial, or lifetime. "I tend to think of home ranges as perennial," Larry Aumiller adds. "The McNeil River sanctuary is

Left: *When salmon are plentiful, dominant bears command the prime McNeil Falls fishing locations. Secondary fishing sites downstream from the falls attract subordinate bears.* **Inset:** *Accompanied by her three yearlings, an adult female named Anita scans the shallow water for salmon. By this age, cubs sometimes attempt to catch fish but are quite inept in their efforts. Cubs often wrest whole fish away from their mother.*

Salmon are most vulnerable in the white water sluicing around the exposed bedrock of McNeil Falls.

The world's largest concentration of bears—sixty-seven have been seen near the falls at one time—prompted the creation of the sanctuary.

really too small to encompass any single bear's lifetime home range. It's only four to five miles wide and twenty-five miles long. Not enough space for a bear."

Because the sanctuary is only a portion of multiple home ranges, it cannot really be said that the sanctuary has a population of one hundred bears, for example. Some bears are predictable, perennial users of the sanctuary, a few appear sporadically, and others show up once and never again. In order to get an accurate count of the sanctuary population, every bear would have to be marked in some fashion. Aumiller estimates that 120 to 150 bears visit McNeil sanctuary from June to September.

Almost all bears that come into the sanctuary are attracted to the McNeil Falls. And it is here the bears come into this atypical contact with each other in order to exploit the rich food source of salmon.

"What's rather surprising about bears," Aumiller remarks, "is that when they are forced to have a social system, one appears. It appears to be simple, geared more toward safety and avoidance than confrontation, but it is there and works quite well."

Researchers in the 1970s studied the encounters between brown bears at McNeil Falls; they recorded how often the bears interacted and what kind of interactions the bears engaged in. Researchers were especially interested in agonistic encounters, or all the aggressive and submissive behavior the bears showed in this unusual gathering. Most often, the bears simply avoided each other, or one bear withdrew when another approached. More intense interactions, such as threat displays, direct charges, and physical contact occurred less frequently.

According to the initial research, large males were avoided by most all other bears, and consequently observers noted few direct interactions involving large males. These dominant males claimed choice fishing locations. Females with cubs were highly intolerant of other bears. These females deferred consistently only to large males. Single adult females showed somewhat more tolerance of other bears than females with cubs. Subadult females and males were least aggressive of all. These subadults were involved in very few aggressive encounters because they generally avoided most other bears. Subadults, however, exhibited aggressive interactions within their own age group.

Status relationships were apparent and ranged, top to bottom, from the dominant adult males to the subor-dinate subadult males. Status among the bears was relatively stable but fluid. A high-ranking individual could back down from a specific encounter, or be run off by an "equal," but still retain a general dominance over that particular animal. According to researchers, subadult bears must make the greatest adjustment in behavior to be able to function within the congregation. Aggression seemed higher in years when salmon runs were diminished, and less when salmon were adequate to abundant for the number of bears congregated at the falls.

Yet, the 1991 chum salmon run on McNeil River was very poor, according to Stonorov, and nevertheless large males were very tolerant of one another. It was a reminder that there are no absolutes in the realm of animal behavior. As Stonorov observes, "Obviously, with such a high density of bears in such a small area, the development of a stable social organization is highly advantageous to minimize fighting and maximize fishing time, especially important when salmon runs are poor or sites are limited by low water."

Bears operate in rather broad ways, with subtle body language nearly nonexistent. Bears don't have the variety of expressive facial features available to wolves or coyotes but instead employ a number of body postures to communicate with other bears. Gait, as well as head and body stance, is used to signal intent.

Bears do use their limited facial features, open mouths, and ears, along with other gestures, to convey aggressive intent. Often these signals are unidentifiable except at close range.

Some experts believe that eye contact between bears also stimulates aggression. They advise people to avoid eye contact with a bear because it can be a provocation. Aumiller doesn't agree. "I don't think eye contact itself is a big part of the message. Bears have rather gross body language signals. Unlike wolves, which are very social animals and have tails to wag, ears that turn in many positions, and facial muscles that can offer a variety of expressions, bears have tiny ears, stubby tails, small eyes, and few facial expressions, all of which don't offer much information at any distance. They also skip a lot of the intervening steps that other animals display prior to aggression simply because they have fewer tools in their body language repertory."

Bears also communicate with sound. Their vocalizations appear to be merely variations of the same sound.

Four large males fished in close proximity at McNeil Falls and occupied prime fishing sites. When one male passed too close to his neighbor, the stress created by their proximity exploded into serious fighting.

The altercation attracted the other two large males.

"Adults make a few sounds that are only mature versions of the cubs' vocalizations," Aumiller explains.

Spring cubs are only comfortable when they are close to their mother, Aumiller points out, and maternal females appear to be relaxed only when cubs are at their side, or in a known position. "In the uncommon situation when a female willingly leaves her cubs, for example to go fishing, she will note their location, keep regular visual tabs on them, and expect them to be there when she returns. When the bond between mother and young breaks, or is threatened, vocalizations occur. Cubs utter a distress call—a hoarse bark similar to that of a fox—and the more distressed they are, the louder they cry. The female responds with a loud call, something of an adult version of the sound the cubs make. However, this "cub call," as it is sometimes termed, may not be a cub summons at all, but a more general fright response.

"I sense that the female realizes the context of the situation has changed and the cubs aren't where they are supposed to be. Suddenly she is stressed by their absence, and in response she gives out a loud woof, or huff. The female continues to utter this sound until she finds her cubs and stops only as her stress dissipates. It is the same sound she makes in several different stressful situations. If cubs hear that noise, it makes them nervous, and when they are nervous, they close ranks. So it has the effect of being a cub call because they come running in response

to it."

Vocalizations can speed the reconnection of mothers and cubs. Often distress calls also can provoke other females and cubs that may be nearby. Female response mechanisms seem easily provoked. Separation followed by a distress call can elicit lightning response in a maternal female.

Of all the senses that the mother may employ to locate her cub, smell is the most important unless she can hear the cub calling. Bears have a well-developed sense of smell, and it usually presents little problem for a female who has lost a cub to actually track it by smell. This task is made more difficult if the cub has crossed a river or other waterway.

A spring cub's in-bred need to stay close to its mother helps it to stay alive. About 35 percent of all cubs do not survive their first year, and 60 percent of all cubs fail to make it to the separation age of two and a half. Clearly it is a dangerous world for bear cubs, and they need mom's protection and "wisdom."

As cubs age, they develop more self-assurance and are allowed more freedom. They wander a bit farther and spend more time away from mother. They appear a little more comfortable on their own. Neither adult nor cub is inclined to respond as quickly to the same stress stimuli as in earlier days. It is a normal, predictable progression toward eventual independence.

Although the two newcomers did not join in the fight, their presence affected its outcome because the male at a disadvantage also had to face off yet another threat.

Facing down the new threat, the loser of the initial fight evidences a gaping wound.

Bears also growl, but describing it as a "warning" is not accurate, Aumiller says. "Usually it is the defending animal, not the aggressor, that's making most of the noise. It could be a warning, but it could also be for intimidation, or distress. Again it seems stress related. Fish stealing usually provokes a lot of growling. The loser makes the noise."

The "bawl" that is commonly associated with bears in movie sound tracks is never heard at McNeil. Aumiller even goes so far as to say brown bears do not make that sound. "The only time I ever heard such a sound was in a French movie. It was the bedroom scene, and it didn't have any bears in it at all."

AGGRESSION AT THE FALLS TENDS TO BE HIGHER THAN ON THE grass flats. Competition for fish brings bears into closer, more volatile contact than during the mellow-paced life associated with spring grazing. Females with cubs, both at the falls and elsewhere, top the list in aggressive behaviors. The trigger is almost always related to distance—another bear's proximity to cubs builds stress. In contrast, the formidable large males seem quite nonaggressive in comparison. "I've had an intense charge by a large male only once," Aumiller recalls, "and I believe that to be rather rare behavior."

Females with cubs are definitely more uncomfort-able at the falls and almost always avoid large males. However, exceptions do occur. In 1991, Molly, a young, inexperienced female with her first litter, fished "elbow to elbow" with the dominant males. This atypical behavior had tragic consequences when her two cubs were killed by two separate bears, one a large male. The gender of the second killer was unknown.

Females with cubs are sometimes, but not always, tolerant of other females with cubs. A behavior documented at the falls that must be considered quite rare is the phenomenon of "adoption," or "cub-swapping."

Alaska Fish and Game employees Al Erickson and Lee Miller were the first to notice this "cub-swapping." On July 22, 1961, a large familiar female was observed fishing at the falls with her three spring cubs. A smaller female, also with three spring cubs, appeared and soon was fishing excitedly near the first female. While the two females were fishing in proximity, the litters of similar-sized cubs mingled. A few minutes later, the smaller female caught a fish and ran up into the alders to eat it. The larger female became agitated for some reason and approached the group of cubs and inspected them. Appearing uncertain of their identity, her stress level increased. She moved downstream about four hundred yards and, followed by all six cubs, crossed the river. She then made her way back up river to a point opposite the place where she had found the six young together.

When the smaller female returned and found her cubs gone, she grew quite agitated and immediately searched the area. Eventually she trailed the cubs downstream and swam across the river at the same point as had the extended family. She then followed the scent trail to the cubs, but the larger female attacked her. During the altercation, one of the cubs fell into the water and was swept away. Both females noticed the cub's plight and went to its aid. The smaller female reached the cub first and helped it to shore and led it out of sight into the alders.

Apparently the smaller female did not regain contact with her other two cubs. When the observers left the sanctuary on August 4, the larger female still had five cubs. It appeared to the observers that the females were either quite tolerant of strange cubs or that they had difficulty in identifying their own. Since the foster female showed up alone in 1962, survival of the "adopted" cubs and even of her own cubs is unknown. Possibly the cubs later reconnected with their own mother. Possibly not.

Tom Bledsoe reported extensive "cub-swapping" in 1974. Red Collar and her five cubs, if indeed this was the original litter size, often fished side by side with Goldie and her two cubs. The litters would mingle much in the same way as those observed in 1961. When Goldie caught a fish and rushed up the bank to eat it, all seven cubs followed her. Usually she returned to the river in a short time, but on occasion she nursed the seven cubs before going back to fish.

Over a period of several days, it was common to see Goldie, Red Collar, and another female, Lady Bird, fishing together at the preferred site. Lady Bird had three cubs of her own. Because the river was low and fishing sites constricted, the females were brought even closer together and their cubs were in constant contact. The

When salmon are scarce a bear will often try to steal a salmon from a subordinate bear, sometimes ripping it from the other's jaws.

cubs then huddled together because of the proximity of other bears. The litters routinely mixed behind their mothers. Often all ten cubs would huddle together or sleep together in a heap. Because the cubs often left with the wrong female, Bledsoe believed that they had little ability to recognize their own mother.

The stress created by the congregation of bears appeared to make the cubs more willing to follow a female away from the river, even if it wasn't their own mother. Bledsoe explains in his book *Brown Bear Summer* that cub-swapping should be termed "sow-swapping" because it appeared the cubs made the decision to trail a different female.

Once all ten cubs were seen with Goldie. She was also seen nursing nine cubs at once. Bledsoe observed a near "adoption" when Goldie had two of Red Collar's cubs for three days. She nursed and protected them without discrimination. Bledsoe's first observation came July 21 and ended on August 6 when the salmon run died out. It appears that the adults did have some ability to recognize their offspring, as each female ended the summer with their own litters mostly intact. At the end of the summer, however, Goldie still had one of Red Collar's cubs. The following year she showed up with just one yearling, having lost two.

Aumiller has seen this "temporary adoption," as he prefers to call it, on four or five different occasions over the last sixteen years. In no other year was the cub mingling as common as in 1974. Once he saw a female with cubs respond to two spring cubs that had no accompanying female, but for some reason the group did not bond, and an actual "adoption" failed to occur. At the falls in 1991, Aumiller saw a spring cub switch temporarily to a female without a cub. Although unaccompanied, the lone female appeared to be lactating. As seems typical of these situations, the cub followed the lone female as she left the river with a fish. The cub then returned to the river still following the "wrong" female. Soon it reconnected with its mother.

Cub mingling is rather rare, according to Aumiller, and is the outgrowth of the unique circumstance of having familiar females fishing side by side. In all cases, these adoptions or "cub-swappings" have been short-lived and often occurred with a complicating event, such as the catch of a fish by one of the females involved. "The events following a capture of a salmon were the critical factor in cub-swapping," Bledsoe agrees.

Animals that raise their young in relative isolation often have limited ability to distinguish their own young from others. Many birds, for example, will rear any young hatched in their nest. However, herd animals, such as caribou, have a powerful ability to identify their own offspring and do not tolerate the young of other female caribou. Brown bear females normally don't have to identify their cubs, as do more social animals, so it can be surmised that their ability to differentiate may be minimal.

To casual observers, it appears that in searching for the best fishing sites, bears move freely about the falls, first to one side, then to the other. In reality there are three broad categories of fishing bears and their behaviors: bears that stay on only the far side of the river, bears that stay on only the near side, and bears that fish both sides of the falls. The determining factor is most often each individual bear's tolerance to humans.

The viewing pad, on a slight rise above the river, and adjacent to the falls, brings bears and people into rather close proximity. First-time, or casual visitors, who may have an inherent unease around bears, often fail to realize that it is they, the humans, who merely by their presence are profoundly influencing the dynamic of perhaps fifty bears.

"On the far side of the river, away from the people on the viewing pad, group all the human-intolerant males," explains Aumiller. "In turn, certain types of bears avoid that far side because of those big males. This avoidance places the females with cubs in one place, the subordinates another. One class of bears displaces another that in turn displaces yet another."

Biologist Colleen Matt points out that the general groupings might be age related. Some bears that stay on the far side were adults when they first came into contact with humans at the sanctuary. They were forced to make a decision about how close they wanted to come to people, and some felt comfortable only on the far side of the river. The separation, she says, may not be determined merely by gender—males here, females there—but by age and experience. A few adult males that grew up in the sanctuary around people are now appearing on the near side of the river. "In the past it was safe to estimate

A young male—facing viewer—is attacked by an adult female (with cubs not pictured) when the two inadvertently ended up in close proximity while fishing.

Bears have several gestures they use to defuse a confrontation. Serious fights are rare, but when they do occur they are almost always brief yet spectacular.

that if there were fourteen males on the far side," Aumiller adds, "twelve of them would stay only there and not come over to the near side. No longer is that so true."

Avoidance of stress-inducing situations is a behavioral mechanism of all bears. Play, on the other hand, even though it can mimic serious fighting, results from the absence of stress. "Generally play is an action rather than a reaction," Aumiller explains, "and not stress related. Stressed bears will not play, but they may fight.

"Bears generally play only with equal-sized partners. Size is a more important factor than age in choosing a play partner. Because males are larger, usually, than females, bears often play within the same gender. A bear that wants to play must find another bear of the same size with the same interest. Some times a smaller bear will show some interest in playing but likely will be uncomfortable with its larger partner. A bear that does involve itself in play with a bigger bear is often easily agitated and will break off the bout. Sometimes the smaller bear must react quite aggressively and forcefully to break off the encounter."

Most authorities agree that maternal females do not play with adult males. In 1981, however, Dick Sellers observed a female named Waif leave her three yearlings on the bank, to move into the pool below the falls to play with an adult male, Flashman. Their play bout was not extended, but nonetheless was unusual.

Potential for great variation exists when bears play. More than two bears could be involved, especially in family groups. Play can occur in water as well as on land. One bear may chase another, catch up to it, wrestle a while; then both resume the chase. The most common form of play involves two young bears. They meet, mouth at one another's head and shoulders, then rear to their hind legs and grapple at one another with mouths and paws. Sometimes they embrace in a dancelike test of strength. They feint at one another with open mouths and occasionally bite one another and take hold of the face, ears, or neck and tug. Sometimes a playful bear will clamber up onto its opponent from behind and grab a mouthful of neck fur, a position very similar to the copulatory pose. All bites and most swats are gentle, but if one bear overdoes it, the other breaks off the play session. Because of the differences in strength, almost al-

Even unrelated young bears spend a lot of time playing.

Above: *Of any age group, spring cubs spend the most time playing. Sometimes mother becomes a willing participant in play, especially when she has an odd number of cubs. Single cubs regularly play with their mother.* **Left:** *Younger bears tend to play more often than older bears, but some continue to play even into their twenties.*

Bears are curious about almost everything they encounter, edible or otherwise.

These cubs have found a fishing float that has washed up on a high tide. It holds their interest for several playful moments.

Play can occur in the water as well as on land. The only requirement for two bears to play seems to be that both bears need to feel comfortable with one another. This almost always means the bears must be of similar size. Large bears sometimes approach smaller ones with a body signal to play, but the smaller bears usually back away or break off contact after a few seconds' tussle.

ways only equal-sized bears engage in play.

Bears at play are usually well-fed bears. Nutrition, as Aumiller points out, influences what a bear does on a minute-to-minute basis. If it is well fed, it is free to pursue other activities such as play. Quite possibly a bear with a full stomach may simply be more comfortable and therefore more likely to play. "It was a huge assumption on my part in 1991 that linked lack of fish to lack of play, but when I thought about the situation objectively, it is apparent that early in the season we see very little play, and later on, after the bears are sated on fish, there's a great deal of play. Of course, this could also be influenced by bears refamiliarizing themselves with one another."

As bears age, they play less frequently. Generally, very old bears just do not play at all. Bear behaviors vary, however. At age eighteen, Rusty, a large male, displayed play behavior that hadn't been seen from him in years. Bears over twenty-five seldom, if ever, play.

Play, in the classic definition of animal behaviorists, is "incomplete behavior." For example, mounting in subadults is incomplete copulation. Play in young animals is often explained as practice of survival skills.

Perhaps play is also one of the many social behaviors of the dominance hierarchy. Generally, it is true that the biggest males have few rivals, but not always are the biggest bears in all sex and age categories dominant in all situations. There are many factors that are involved, and maybe play, very rough play, is one of them.

A few big males have what Aumiller calls an "attitude" and in these unique cases, their rivals are nonexistent. "Charlie Brown and Dismay were two that had an

Bears often amuse themselves by playing with their own feet or a nearby object. Even an old spawned-out salmon can be fun.

'attitude.' I've seen just enough of their demeanor to know that they can't be pushed. If they want something, they take it. You can almost see it in the way they walk to the fishing sites. Their steps seem to imply: 'I don't care if you've got one hundred cubs, outta my way.' They are just a little more aggressive than other bears."

When one of the typical males arrives on the far side of the river, he claims his desired fishing site by displaying just enough dominance to displace other bears. Not so Aumiller's bears with an "attitude."

"When Dismay—like Charlie Brown before him—first arrived on the far side on that first day of each season, he'd walk down to the river, not even attempt to fish, but attack the first male he came to and throw him in the river. Then he'd look at the next one and throw him in the river and so on until he'd cleared the bank. Only then would he go fishing. The next day, the same thing would happen. It didn't take long for the other bears to move off when Dismay showed up on the bluff above the river. The river bank would clear out. Dismay was like a shark going through a school of tuna. There'd always be a big empty space around him devoid of bears

as each bear would move away to keep its distance; then he would fish."

Dominance allows certain bears access to prime fishing sites, and often they quit coming to the falls well before subordinate bears begin to leave. "In the absence of nutritional studies, we have to speculate that they have satisfied a certain nutritional need and are moving on to something else," Aumiller says. "The bears that stick it out into late August are usually the ones that have been excluded from the prime fishing spots early on, or who have added nutritional needs, like females with cubs."

Some bears depart as early as late July, at a time when perhaps the salmon run is still improving. More begin leaving in early August. Possibly they move to another run where the competition—and stress—is less. No one really knows. They are leaving, however, well before the berries are ripe. When the berries do ripen in late August, most bears have left the sanctuary. The drop-off in activity at the falls can be quite sudden and dramatic. One day twenty bears will be there, the next day two. The drama is over for another year.

In a sense the bear-human relationship at McNeil River has been an experiment. This outdoor laboratory is unique in the world, a place where we have learned that bears seem far more willing to get along with people than people are with bears. What occurs within the sanctuary is the human acceptance of the notion that in this place human desires matter little, and that bears come first.

OVER WINTER
INTO SPRING

"DENS ARE USUALLY DUG AT HIGH EL-evations so that deep snow will help maintain a thermal barrier. One spring several years ago, I was sur-prised to find a den quite low and directly behind the campground," Larry Aumiller recalls. "Snow cov-ered the hillside, and I could easily see where a medium-sized bear had dug out and had spent time around the entrance before wandering off. As I approached the den, I noticed fresh tracks, but after hollering and tossing snowballs toward the entrance, I was certain the bear was not there. I walked up for a look. I then crawled part-way in but couldn't see because of the darkness. After looking around the entrance a bit, I headed home.

"The next day, armed only with a flashlight and a camera, I returned to the den. About 125 feet from the hole, I looked down and noticed that my foot prints from the day before had fresh bear prints over them. I froze. I was flooded with an odd mixture of adrenaline rush and euphoria. I turned slowly away and retraced my steps. I know that spring bears are lethargic and sometimes stay at the den for up to two weeks after first emerging, especially if they have new cubs. The cubs of-ten stay in the den while the mother is temporarily away.

"Once I got a couple hundred yards away, and could breathe again, I recognized how lucky I was that I hadn't blundered into a situation that could have been disas-trous. I can only guess what would have happened had I tried to crawl into that den and there was a bear, or a female with cubs, in it. It was really dumb. There was only one way out, and that was over—or through—me."

DO BEARS HIBERNATE? OR IS THEIR WINTER SLEEP A SIMILAR BUT different state some biologists label "winter dormancy"?

In response to cold or famine, a few northern and

Left: *Cubs become insecure when away from their mother, even if she is fishing only a few yards away. Despite the swiftness of the river, cubs often try to follow their mother into the water but when thwarted they maintain visual contact from shore as best they can.* **Inset:** *A passing bear draws the attention of this bear family feeding in tall sedges.*

alpine mammals enter periods of extended sleep, called dormancy. It is not uncommon for dormant animals to awaken and feed or even become active for a while before again falling asleep. Dormant animals experience some physiological change while sleeping but do not experience the profound physiological changes of hibernators. In contrast, true hibernators are capable of voluntarily reducing their metabolic rates and body temperatures for extended periods of time. For example, the arctic ground squirrel can withstand body temperatures lower than freezing for three weeks without its blood freezing. Dormant animals, because their body functions remain near normal, are easily roused from sleep; hibernators are not.

Bears do wake up in winter and sometimes even make short forays. However, black bears and brown bears undergo a form of hibernation that in many respects may be more profound than that of classic hibernators. It takes about two weeks for bears to slip completely into deep sleep. They remain in winter dens from four to seven months, with little movement and without food, water, urination, or defecation. Some bears in Alaska spend 60 percent of their entire lives in the den.

Scientists are investigating the physiological adaptations that allow bears to avoid bone degeneration, waste accumulation, muscle atrophy, and dangerous chemical imbalance during this period of prolonged inactivity. Because of their thick layer of fat, insulative fur, and reduced blood flow to the extremities, hibernating bears can maintain normal core temperatures while burning calories at only half their usual rate. Although their heart rates in the den are just 25 percent to 45 percent of summer rates, their body temperatures decline only 7 degrees Fahrenheit. "Bradycardia," as slow heart rate is termed, is associated with circulatory shunting, which continues normal blood flow to heart, lungs, and brain, but only minimal support for other organ systems. Recent comparisons of cardiac function place bears with true hibernators, thus ending the confusion with such terms as *dormancy*.

Some brown bears den in excavations at the foot of trees in old-growth forests, a very few dig snow dens, and rarely a few overwinter in shallow depressions in the ground. Most brown bears usually excavate their own dens. On Admiralty Island in Southeast Alaska, one study revealed that natural crevices and caves were the

Above: *When bears emerge from their dens in early May, winter still grips Kamishak country. In another month the snow will be gone and the hills and flats will be greening up. This period just after hibernation is thought to be the time of greatest natural mortality for bears. Their fat layers are exhausted, and precious little forage is available to them.* **Inset:** *Prior to, and sometimes even after, actual mating, bears relate to one another in lengthy, ritualized ways. Much of the behavior display depends upon the female's receptivity to the male.*

most frequent type of den, which is not typical for North American brown bears. Over most of Alaska, however, annual excavations, like the one Aumiller tried to investigate, are the norm.

Brown bears apparently do not reuse excavated dens. In Southeast Alaska, however, rock cavities were reused by two females for up to perhaps three consecutive years. On the southwest side of Kodiak Island, several instances of cave dens being reused were documented. Two females used their same den sites for five consecutive winters. No cave dens have been found in the McNeil sanctuary.

Most inland bears tend to den at elevations above one thousand feet on north-facing slopes, where snow accumulation is greatest and unaffected by winter solar heating. The thermal barrier created by the snow protects hibernating bears from extreme weather. Dens have been found from sea level to altitudes of several thousand feet. Elevation and exposure variations occur due to local conditions. The den Aumiller found was just three hundred feet above sea level and one quarter mile from tidewater. In interior Alaska, temperatures may drop to as low as a record -80 degrees Fahrenheit. Adequate snow-cover may be of paramount importance to denning success there. Winter temperatures at McNeil of -20 degrees Fahrenheit, and colder, are not uncommon, nor are winds of 60 miles per hour, and more.

To den, brown bears travel to the same general area that they used the previous winter. Biologists describe the den digging process as fairly low-key and interspersed with extended rest periods. Bears often make several excavations in adjacent locations before completing a den. Excavated dens are surprisingly small. Usually a tunnel leads straight inward about three to four feet to the bedding chamber, often hardly large enough for the bear. The undisturbed root mass around the fresh excavation may make the den itself more stable and perhaps warmer. Constant subfreezing den temperatures are important for maintaining den integrity. Most earth dens tend to collapse in the spring as the ground thaws.

One spring, Aumiller and two friends skied from Kulik Lake, on the west side of the Chigmit Mountains, to the camp at McNeil River. On the three-day trip in late April, they saw four open dens with tracks around them, and two bears. All the sites were on south- and east-facing slopes, with only one actually in the sanctu-

ary. The bear at that site saw the skiers but did not react.

Denning begins in the McNeil area in mid-October. Aumiller has remained at the sanctuary into early November. His last verified bear sighting in McNeil Cove was on October 23. (Denning time and duration vary across Alaska's mix of habitats and microclimates.) Early naturalists believed that the trigger for hibernation was the onset of cold weather and snow. Now we know that many bears enter the den long before snow is on the ground, and some remain out despite it. Speculation currently centers on a combination of factors: food availability, diminishing daylight, weather, and perhaps most importantly, the physical condition of the individual bear. The disappearance of abundant high-quality food items, like silver salmon, may be the key factor that sends bears into their den. Studies have been conducted with captive bears—hibernation can be triggered by a cessation of winter feeding.

"The few dens I've seen in the McNeil area," Jim Faro says, "were close to areas that supported late fall silver salmon runs. Most were to the south and quite close to such streams." Faro has seen bears in December feeding on silver salmon on the Savonoski River in Katmai National Park, with two feet of snow on the ground. He believes the rich food source was delaying their hibernation.

Females generally enter their dens earlier than males and emerge later. Pregnant females enter the den earliest of all. Adult females with first-year cubs den next, then females with older cubs, followed by unpregnant, unaccompanied females. Next to enter are subadult bears of both sexes. The last to den are mature males. It is not unheard of to find large males out as late as November or December, or emerging in early April. On Kodiak, biologists Larry Van Daele and Roger Smith found that more than 25 percent of the collared males in their Terror Lake study area did not hibernate at all. These males who did not den were sedentary and lethargic, a condition they called "walking hibernation."

Spring emergence tends to be in reverse order to den entrance: first, large males; then, single females, subadults, females with older cubs; and last, females with spring cubs. Snow and cold can delay spring emergence. The first bears that turn up in the sanctuary in the spring are almost always single adult bears.

Spring may be the time of highest mortality for bears.

In the sanctuary it is not unusual to see a second, less-dominant male near a breeding pair. However, it is uncommon to have a second estrous female on the periphery of a breeding pair, as seen here.

On the gravels of Mikfik Creek, Dave, a young male, breeds with Teddy. Two days later Teddy also breeds with Woofie, a huge male. Copulation typically lasts thirty to forty minutes.

Above: *After mating, which can occur several times over the span of several days, it is common for both bears to rest together. Here Dave has mated with another female, Barni, and the pair is about to lie down for rest.* **Right:** *Although bears no doubt absorb water from the foods they eat, they do drink water quite often, especially on warm days.*

Until recently it was believed that the highest bear mortality occurred during denning. However, Sterling Miller's radio-telemetry research leads to speculation that the greatest mortality occurs just after bears leave the den. At the time of emergence, snow covers the ground and food is not readily available. Bears are starting to use energy at a higher rate. Intake often is lower than output, and that disparity, coupled with nearly exhausted fat reserves, pushes bears to the edge of survival, making them vulnerable.

MATING SEASON FOR BROWN BEARS RUNS FROM MAY THROUGH early July, with the peak in June. Breeding activity has been observed at McNeil as late as August 10, the latest seen in North America.

Males are attracted to females in estrus; primarily by smelling the scent the females leave. Females leave scent in their urine or by contacting the ground or vegetation with their bodies, which are also scented with urine. Scent also may be carried on the wind. Males, their noses to the ground like bloodhounds, have been seen several times following exactly in the steps of estrous females. Upon contact, the female's behavior then provides the male with further information on her receptivity. Females not in estrus grow quite apprehensive at a male's approach, sometimes fleeing at a dead run. Unless displaced by a more dominant male, a male once having found a near-estrous female will continue to follow her, no matter how complex her evasive techniques.

If the female on first encounter does run away, the male will keep at a distance until she is ready to accept him at closer range. Both by her response to his approach and by scent, the male tests the female's receptivity hour by hour, or even moment by moment. He moves in, she moves away. He moves in, she moves away. Each time he may be allowed to get closer, but actual contact is avoided. It is a cycle of pursuit and testing that often is subtle, merely one bear slowly ambling about the hillside, followed at an unvarying distance by another. Once in awhile the pursuit is more energetic.

"Once we saw a female coming down the beach toward camp, with a male tagging along a short distance behind," Aumiller recalls. "They were moving rapidly, though not quite at a run, the male matching the female's pace. Coming in front of camp, the female rounded the

inside of the curved gravel spit and actually doubled back on the male, passing quite close to him. She was on one side of the spit, he was on the other. He looked over the spit and saw her at close range, but he literally stayed right on her tracks taking the much longer route. In this case even though he could see her, he seemed to trust only his sense of smell and continued on in her exact footsteps, nose to the ground."

Eventually the female becomes more receptive. Her normal unease lessens until she is quite approachable. Soon the two are grazing and resting in close proximity. Instead of avoidance, the female allows contact, nuzzling and even minimal play. This type of play is unlike the play associated with mating behavior. Two bears that are comfortable with one another roll around, grappling each other with their forelegs, while gently biting one another on the face, neck, and shoulders. The pair graze close to one another, even nap together. The male may try to mount the female, but at this stage she is not yet receptive and moves away or sits down. This precopulatory behavior, a low-level testing, may continue for several days.

Copulation, when it occurs, seems to last about forty-five minutes. Penetration is possible through the aid of a baculum, or penis bone, which, instead of blood engorgement, provides erection. Sometimes the copulation lasts over an hour, or as little as just a few seconds.

Copulation may at times involve a fair bit of aggression on the female's part. If the male mounts and she's not quite ready, or if he's too aggressive, she will reach around and bite or attack the male. Her roaring assault can be quite spectacular, never failing to impress both the male and any humans who may be watching.

After mating, there is a discernible lessening of tension between the pair. In time the tension again builds up, and the whole mating ritual is repeated. "The pair's demeanor changes after copulating," Aumiller reports. "They break apart and need to rest up. They may nuzzle and sleep draped on one another."

They may copulate on and off for three or four days before the female suddenly appears uncomfortable with the male's presence and moves away. Fertilization of an egg or eggs has taken place, cessation of estrus is rather abrupt: The bears part quickly.

Large, dominant males do most of the breeding. Within the space of a few weeks, each male might mate

Left: *Undisturbed nursing bouts usually last from six to eight minutes. Older cubs, because they are more efficient at suckling, nurse for shorter periods. Here Teddy nurses her spring cubs.* **Above:** *Ms. Mouse nurses her three spring cubs. Bears have four nipples on their chest and two on their lower abdomen. Cubs make a loud purring sound while nursing.*

with four or five, or more, females. Sexual maturation for males is six and a half years, but these inexperienced young males are easily displaced by older bears. Sometimes, however, mating is circumstantial. Bears are not territorial; they share overlapping home ranges. Even though dominant males may be in the area, a younger male that happens on to an estrus female will breed with her.

PRIOR TO HIBERNATION, BEARS GO ON AN AUTUMNAL BINGE OF feeding, called "hyperphagia," and load on the fat. A bear's general physical condition and predenning accumulation of fat reserves are critical for overwinter survival. Berries, an important autumnal food item, are consumed into late autumn. A bear can get waddling fat just eating berries, but a late run of silver salmon can be important. Once the optimum level of fat is achieved, a growing lethargy sends bears to their den. In healthy bears, only fat is burned during hibernation, not protein. Loss of muscle mass is the effect of starvation.

Physical condition is all important for denning females and profoundly affects reproductivity and cub survival. After breeding in the spring, a female may carry from one to six fertilized eggs, or zygotes. In bears, zygote growth stalls at an early developmental stage. The blastocyst, as the zygote is termed at this stage, does not attach to the uterine wall immediately as is the usual process in most other mammals, but floats free in the uterus. This developmental suspension, termed "delayed implantation," continues until about the time of denning, when the blastocyst attaches to the uterine wall and normal gestation begins. Blastocysts will not implant unless there is a certain level of nutritional success, which appears to be tied to fall feeding rather than summer or spring feeding. In nutritionally stressed females, reproduction takes second place to survival. In starving animals, the blastocyst dissolves, or later, the fetuses are resorbed.

Faro speculates that delayed implantation allows bears to maximize their reproductive success. Several eggs can be fertilized in the spring at a time when the future food source is undetermined. If the season is good, and the female is in top shape, her body allows multiple blastocysts to develop. If the season is poor, and the female in marginal condition, then no blastocysts develop, which aids the survival of the female through the winter.

Since the breeding season lasts weeks, with insemination dates and actual birth dates unknown, biologists in Alaska have assigned the date January 1, as bears' generic "birth date." In reality, cubs are born over a several-day period in midwinter, depending upon the time of blastocyst attachment. All spring cubs—biologists call them "cubs of the year"—are therefore one half year old upon arrival at McNeil River in the spring.

The birth process is quite low-key. The female just barely stirs before drifting back into hibernation for what could be three or four more months. Sometimes the female wakes up and assists the birth. The tiny cubs, less than a pound each, enter the world with little trauma. The cubs are born blind, naked, and helpless—essentially premature—but they don't require all that much from their mother. At the least, a female must be healthy enough to adequately supply milk and warmth. There is speculation that the female licks her nipples, making a trail for the cubs to follow, a process similar to what a kangaroo does for its young so that they may find their way to the nipples in the pouch. A female bear's belly is almost hairless, and when the mother is curled into fetal position a natural warm pocket develops.

The growth rate of the cubs is initially very slow. Nursing cubs in essence are robbing their mother of her vital nutrients, and for her survival, the nutrient drain must be at a low level. Cubs gain about two pounds a month and weigh ten to twelve pounds upon emergence. Spring cubs usually emerge from the den by the second or third week in May when they are four to five months old. A female may emerge with up to four cubs. Six is the record number. Over the last several years, McNeil litters have averaged 2.2 cubs.

THE PATTERN OF EMERGENCE FROM THE DEN VARIES WIDELY, depending on age and sex of the individual bear. Bears do not simply wake up, climb out of the den, and gallop off. The energy drain would be substantial.

A bear typically opens the den by forcing its head out through the snow cover. It then may look around before crawling back into the den. A few minutes, hours, or even days later, it may look out again. Perhaps it comes part way out of the den or all the way out. It may

Teeny is the smallest adult female at McNeil River. All female brown bears are protective of their cubs. Surprisingly, cubs seem to have a limited ability to recognize their own mothers. In rare situations cubs have joined with an unrelated female and cubs.

Melody rears up on her hind legs in an attempt to locate her cubs. Separation of females and cubs is a high stress situation for adult and offspring alike.

Above: As she comes into estrus, Melody turns on her own two-and-a-half-year-old cubs in an attempt to drive them away. Separation between mother and cubs can be a violent episodic event lasting over several hours, or even days. **Right:** Siblings will often stay together after separating from their mother. Because they are often very shy of other bears they go to great lengths to avoid them, sometimes climbing steep cliffs, up onto rocks, or swimming rivers to get away.

Two yearlings await their mother's return from a fishing foray, warily watching the passage of another bear. As summer progresses females with cubs feed incessantly as they prepare themselves and cubs for the approaching winter.

take a few steps, turn around a time or two, then crawl back into the den. Or it may nap at the mouth of the den. Short forays may soon ensue. Tracks and trails soon radiate in all directions.

If the den contains cubs, a day or so will pass before one is seen. The cubs might lie at the entrance with the female, or wander a few awkward steps. Their motor skills are poor; there is little, if any, play. If the weather turns bad, the whole family will retreat to the den, sometimes for days. Eventually the bears spend several consecutive days above ground, and they abandon the den. The long winter sleep is over.

Biologist Sterling Miller believes that the delay in moving to lower elevations increases survivorship of newborn litters by minimizing predation by other bears. Accidents, like drownings, also claim many spring cubs. Even in midsummer, spring cubs are at risk when crossing McNeil River, for example. In Miller's study, females accompanied by newborn cubs who moved to lower elevations soon after emergence appeared to lose their cubs more often than females that remained at higher elevations.

Females with cubs typically avoid contact with other bears. They prefer protected areas, with good visibility, where other bears are unlikely to be found. High talus slopes that melt off sooner than other areas and that may provide overwintered berries or emerging vegetation are preferred sites for females with cubs. Winter carrion or washed up marine mammals on occasion may provide a feeding bonanza. Family groups usually avoid choice feeding zones because other bears concentrate there. Following especially harsh winters, when spring food is scarce, bears are drawn together in competition for limited available food. In such cases, it may be difficult for a female with cubs to avoid other bears as well as obtain enough to eat.

One spring, Larry Aumiller and I walked the coast from Illiamna Bay to McNeil River, a distance of roughly ninety miles. We observed a female and two two-year-old cubs walking across a sheer cliff above tidewater. They were two hundred feet up in a spot more suitable for mountain sheep than bears. Rocks tumbled down the cliff at each step, and we feared that one of the cubs would fall. This was a graphic example of the extreme places a female will take her cubs in order to avoid other bears.

Females with spring cubs show up almost a month after the first lone bears arrive on the sanctuary sedge flats. These family groups tend to segregate themselves as much as possible from other bears. They prefer areas of unhindered visibility with open escape routes. Some stay near the protection of the conglomerate bluffs that border McNeil Cove which is inundated daily by the tides. Subadult bears also prefer these open areas for about the same reasons. Females with cubs tend to remain in the open sedge flats well after the other bears have begun to cluster around McNeil Falls. Only later in the season will they venture to the falls, and then with caution.

In contrast, large males seek out heavy cover, apparently more comfortable in areas of limited visibility. After the bears have left in the fall, Aumiller has examined the area around the falls and located dozens of well-worn day beds in the densest alder thickets. Most are on the far side of the river, but some are surprisingly close to the viewing pad or human trail.

Spring cubs stay quite close to their mother and watch her behaviors closely. Their senses improve daily, as do their motor skills. Play takes up an increasing portion of their time. Despite their "baby teeth," these small cubs begin to graze almost at once upon arriving on the sedge flats. Though the tough sedges appear quite challenging, spring cubs graze voraciously despite the lack of molars.

The sedge flats extend along the banks of Mikfik Creek as it winds its way to the cove. As summer approaches, this low-lying acreage turns to an ocean of green, providing the first widely available food for bears. The flats are profoundly affected by the sea whose high tides flood them. By midsummer, the sedges are three feet high and offer both food and cover to bears. The sedges' whispering in the near-constant winds are persistent summer and autumn sounds.

Much of a young bear's nutrition continues to come from mother's milk. The younger the bear, the more often it nurses. Spring cubs nurse about every two to three hours. Weight gain in spring cubs initially is not rapid.

"Cubs almost always initiate the nursing sequence,"

Aumiller reports. "Nearly 100 percent of the time, they signal their desire to nurse. Cubs signal their readiness by vocalizing and assuming a certain demeanor. The nursing vocalization is somewhat similar to their distress call, a short, staccato bleat that rises in volume and rapidity as levels of distress or need rise. Nursing bouts often follow a stressful situation, or something traumatic. An interaction with another bear, a chase, a separation, or an accident, like a cub being swept over the falls, for example, will invariably trigger a bout. Once we saw a spring cub that was separated from its mother for over an hour, and it started calling, practically screaming. You could hear it for hundreds of yards. Eventually the two reunited, and nursing was the first thing on the agenda."

In a scenario that takes place in many species of mammals, the begging cubs move in on their mother and attempt to get under her and take hold of a nipple. If a balance exists between the mother's feeling comfortable (no other bears are nearby, for example) and the cubs' expressing their need, the female will sit down and roll onto her back, legs splayed. Brown bears have six nipples, four on the chest and two between the hind legs; the cubs prefer the nipples on the chest. While nursing the cubs make a loud purring, almost a humming, sound. It is the female who usually breaks off the nursing bout; she either gets up and walks away, or simply rolls over, and the family collapses in a heap for a nap. Sometimes the cubs drain all six sources dry and cease nursing. Following nursing, milk often decorates the cubs' muzzles and chests.

"Humans can relate especially to nursing, to mother and young," Aumiller observes. "It's something I don't think many people see, either in films or pictures, and certainly not up close in the field. Nursing is a behavior these two species, humans and bears, share, although people don't think of nursing in terms of being a 'behavior'—instead they feel a kinship with the bears."

Many magazine articles refer to large males as cub-killers. Over the last sixteen years, however, Larry Aumiller and his colleagues have witnessed only four cases of cubs being killed by other bears, and three have been by females. In one instance described earlier, a yearling became separated from its mother, White, and was killed by another female when the yearling apparently attempted to join her and her two spring cubs.

On another occasion, two adult females were seen

fighting in the water at the mouth of Mikfik Creek. One of them, McBride, had three cubs on a bluff above the lagoon, two-thirds of a mile away. Her antagonist, Fossey, had two spring cubs that stayed close to her despite the struggle. As the fight moved toward shore, the two cubs ran twenty-five yards out onto the mudflat. After reaching shore, McBride chased down and killed one of Fossey's cubs as it tried to rejoin its mother. She then drove off Fossey and killed her second cub.

Visitor Barbara Meyer remembers, "Seeing these cubs get killed was a jolt of reality. Bears being bears. Not cute TV images."

McBride and her three yearlings were involved in another incident a year later. Melody and her two spring cubs were fishing from the sand spit. She would leave her cubs on shore and wade out into the water to fish. At one point, McBride and her three yearlings were seen passing near Melody's cubs. Much of what happened next was hidden from the view of observers. One of Melody's cubs soon was seen running along the spit until out of sight. Melody then moved in the same direction, her nose to the ground, apparently searching for her cub. She soon ran back toward McBride and engaged in a brief fight. After this, Melody ran the opposite way from her cub and crossed the mouth of the river. She then climbed the bluff, apparently searching for her cub. An hour and a half later, Aumiller and colleague Pauline Hessing inspected the fight scene and found the carcass of a male cub by the water's edge. Its neck was broken and its body severely bitten.

Melody continued to search for her cubs and about an hour later located the dead cub on the beach. Throughout the ensuing hours, she continued her search for her second cub, grunting and moaning as she searched the area at a rapid walk. Almost eight hours after the fight, Melody's surviving cub appeared on the beach one-third mile from camp. Melody, now behind camp, heard the cub and trotted to it. After an initial sniffing and inspection, she immediately nursed the cub for five minutes. They then both lay down together for a nap. During the next week Melody's second cub was found dead, possibly as the result of a wound received from another bear.

Another incident was recorded in the summer of 1991. Salmon were scarce and competition for them keen. Directly across from the viewing pad at the falls, in midafternoon, eight-year-old Molly left her two spring cubs on the grassy bank in order to pursue another bear carrying a fish. Molly was in the habit of fishing relatively close to the dominant males. When she was thirty yards from her cubs, a medium-sized male, Pretty Boy, saw them and quickly approached. The alarmed cubs attempted to escape, but one was caught and shaken violently by the back until dead. Pretty Boy carried it in his mouth to the water's edge where he put it down on the rocks in order to sniff and paw it.

Suddenly aware of the missing cubs, Molly approached to within fifteen yards of Pretty Boy before she turned away to resume searching along the bank. Pretty Boy abandoned the carcass almost immediately and wandered downstream. Ten minutes later, he returned and began to eat the dead cub. In his absence, two other males had wandered by to smell the carcass but neither fed upon it. Pretty Boy fed sporadically until only the cub's head and feet remained.

Molly continued to search for her cubs throughout the afternoon, at one point coming within twenty yards of the carcass but not stopping to investigate it. Within thirty seconds of Pretty Boy's attack, the remaining cub was seen in the mouth of another bear on the bluff above the river. In over five thousand hours of observation at the falls, this was the first time Aumiller saw an adult male kill and eat a cub.

Incidents of infanticide generate many questions. There is no universally accepted motivation for cub-killing. Some of the common reasons postulated to explain infanticide by adult males include: sociopathy; food gathering (an adult bear killing a cub with the specific, premeditated goal of eating it); and triggering of the female's estrus cycle by killing the nursing young, which eventually provides a breeding opportunity for the male. The last is the most commonly accepted theory. However, since we as humans cannot explain aberrant behavior within our own species, how can we expect to explain curious behaviors, including infanticide, in other species?

Having one of the lowest reproductive rates of large terrestrial mammals, female brown bears can be expected to invest heavily in the care of their young. Even though they are putting themselves at risk, females with cubs are known to be aggressive toward any bear that comes too close to their cubs. Not all threats from other bears end in the death of cubs. In 1988, the one-thousand-pound

Dismay, the largest male at the falls, attacked one of Teeny's twenty-pound cubs. Although she was only one-third the attacker's size, Teeny's ferocious intervention drove off Dismay. She charged at him, which in turn froze him in his tracks. She pressed her attack, pushing the male with her forelegs and snapping away with her jaws. Each lunge was met with counter-lunge, the male holding ground but not overpowering the smaller female. As her stress level dissipated, the intensity of her attack diminished until she broke off and backed away. Dismay stood, checked, as he watched Teeny move away.

In the aftermath, her wounded cub was unable to keep up with her mother and her two siblings and soon became separated. Helen, a female with three cubs of her own, temporarily "adopted" the wounded cub and was seen nursing all four cubs. A few days later the injured cub appeared with another female, Lanky, and her two spring cubs. Lanky is believed to be Teeny's mother, and therefore the wounded cub's grandmother. Lanky was accompanied by all three cubs when she left the sanctuary two weeks later.

Some biologists suggest that cub-killing by adult males acts to limit bear populations, especially in high-density populations. If true, this relationship suggests that a heavily hunted population may have higher cub survivorship because hunters tend to select for male bears. By law, in Alaska, females with cubs and cubs are protected. Hunters prefer males because they are larger, but many small bears or lone females are also killed. According to area biologist Dick Sellers, 60 percent of all bears killed on the Alaska Peninsula are males. Of the total, males averaged five years old, females six years. However, as events within the sanctuary illustrate, cub mortality also results from attacks by adult females. This suggests that it may be inaccurate to assume that hunting of adult males will result in increased cub survivorship.

Whatever the mortality factor, research by Sellers and Aumiller indicates that sanctuary bears experience poor productivity. According to Sellers, of the eleven sanctuary females that have been followed from sexual maturity to presumed death, each has raised an average of only two cubs through the end of the second summer. Thus for the entire fifteen-year period, 1976 to 1991, the eleven females raised a total of just twenty-two cubs.

Cubs usually stay with their mother until their third spring. Sometime after hibernation the family separates. Unlike mountain sheep, for example, that breed while the female is still accompanied by the yearling, bear families separate prior to females' contact with males. With the onset of estrus, a hormonal change takes place, and the mother simply ceases care of her young. The cubs typically continue to hang around their mother, but she discourages them, even to the point of attacking them.

Aumiller had the opportunity in 1991 to witness for the first time the entire sequence of events in the family separation. In late June, Melody showed up with her two-and-a-half-year-old twins. Aumiller remarks that it was a little late in the spring for her to be still accompanied by cubs of that age. He thought that perhaps she would keep her cubs another summer.

One afternoon on upper Mikfik Creek, Melody and her cubs were fishing in a "normal, unstressed manner," when a more dominant bear appeared and forced the family group up onto a bluff overlooking the creek. Melody and her two cubs were sitting looking down at the bear fishing in their vacated spot, when suddenly Melody put her head down, and growling, moved toward her cubs.

"They didn't know how to respond to this new and unusual behavior except just to look at her," Aumiller recalls. "She then lunged and bit one of her cubs. The cub recoiled into defensive posture. Jaw to jaw they snapped at one another, the second cub cowering behind its sibling. Melody pressed in on the two. The lead cub was just able to fend her off, much like you would see adult bears do if one were trying to steal another's fish. Once she'd forced the cubs down the bank, Melody turned her back and started away. Of course, the cubs followed her just as they had every day of their lives.

"Melody turned and saw them when they topped the bluff behind her. She immediately attacked again, forcing them back down the hill. This time she got fifty feet away before the cubs caught up. As their momentum took them up to her, Melody spun around and violently attacked. Each cub sustained bites to its rump and shoulders.

"One cub seemed to persist. It just couldn't get the message. After a vigorous punishing, however, both cubs did back off. They followed Melody at a distance of about one hundred feet, or so, as she moved down toward the lower riffles. There the cubs attempted to move in, but again Melody attacked them. Each time this happened it took the cubs longer to return to her. By the end of the day, we had seen four or five of these serious encounters between Melody and her cubs. By the next morning, the separation was complete."

Over the course of the next few days whenever the cubs saw or scented Melody, they would move toward her. When they closed to within 100 to 150 feet, Melody would put her head down and assume an aggressive posture. The cubs would slam to a halt, then back off.

Melody was soon in estrus, and over the course of the next two weeks, she was bred by three or four different males. Occasionally the cubs would encounter her, or the mating pair, but made no attempt to get close.

"In the past, we thought that separation was a combination of factors: a weakening maternal bond, onset of estrus, the risk to the cubs presented by an amorous male," Aumiller says. "Now it seems reasonable to assume that separation is a result of hormonal change. It was days before Melody was ready to breed, yet she put out a very clear message to her cubs: 'Don't come near me.'"

This particular event took an even more unusual twist. Following Melody's estrus cycle, and after a two-week separation, Melody and her cubs reunited. Aumiller also witnessed this reconnection. The two cubs, now known as Melba and Carmella, came up on the bluff above the flats and saw Melody fishing on the creek below. They put their heads down and began uttering the call that cubs give when they want to nurse. Melody looked back at them but then returned to fishing. The vocal cubs moved in a little closer. Still Melody did nothing. They sat down fifty feet behind her and continued to whine. They made an effort to approach, but she turned on them. One slipped in

the mud and fell down, and Melody immediately was standing over it, but she did not bite or hurt it. Melody then backed off.

The next day Aumiller went back and found Melody nursing both cubs! "Astounding sight!" he recalls. "Soon Melody began to lactate again and went back to being a mother. But how they actually got close enough to begin that interaction is a mystery. No one knows how often this phenomenon occurs."

Melody and her cubs stayed together throughout the rest of the summer. What happened next was anyone's guess. If Melody hadn't bred that spring, the normal scenario would have been for her to den with her cubs. According to Aumiller, over 80 percent of cubs separate at the start of the third summer, when they are two and a half years old, about 15 percent at three and a half years, and about 5 percent beginning the fifth summer. Since Melody had come into estrus, a fall separation was likely. It seems in such cases that the female senses a change in herself and separates from her cubs to avoid having them in the den with her newborns.

"If you observe an animal long enough, it will contradict every generality in print," Dick Sellers points out. "At McNeil, we have seen very unusual behaviors: a maternal female playing with an adult male; weaning followed by reunion; and females killing cubs. It just proves that every rule has its exception and complexity."

On the Douglas River, just south of McNeil River, in the spring of 1991, Sellers twice saw a litter of mixed-aged cubs. The litter contained two large cubs—perhaps yearlings, or older—and two spring cubs. The second time Sellers flew over, he saw the female nursing all four cubs.

Only during breeding season will females allow large males in close proximity. As the estrus peaks, the female's natural unease around males relaxes and she accepts a close approach. Copulation follows days of fairly close contact, which perhaps even includes bouts of play. Here Earl approaches Norma Jean just prior to copulation.

RIVER OF HOPE

THE LAMBENT LIGHT OF EVENING SLANTS across the shoulders of the Chigmit Mountains and falls upon a family of bears feeding in tall autumnal sedge. A few gulls chorus at the mouth of McNeil River. It is the only sound to be heard above the wind wrestling in the sedge.

Just as the sun dips below the peaks, with the tide ebbing, the loud roar of a floatplane taking off from the cove rends the stillness. The bear family—a female and her two spring cubs—look up from their grazing, but as the sound quickly fades, they lose interest.

A few hundred feet over the bay, the plane makes a turn and circles over the river mouth. Pilot Bill deCreeft and his passenger, Larry Aumiller, take one last look before heading toward Homer. They see just the three bears and no others. Passing over camp, they look down at the cabins boarded up for winter. All the valuable gear is loaded on the plane and bound for winter storage. Gone are the tents and summer visitors. Now, in late September, the sanctuary is solely the domain of the few bears left in it.

Despite having grazed for over an hour, the two spring cubs are hungry. They move in on their mother, demanding to nurse. Slowly she sits down and rolls onto her back. Her twins nudge into her chest and begin to nurse with soft purrings. In the wind, in the chill, and in the sudden silence, she watches her cubs as they suckle. She yawns. And yawns again. Fifteen minutes later, the three bears are sprawled asleep on one another.

In the distance, Augustine vents steam and light ash into the air. A seal surfaces off the spit, just its head breaking the wind-tossed waves. It looks in all directions before quietly submerging again. Tonight the season's first ice will form on the ponds, and waterfowl will continue on their way south. It is the day before winter.

IN THE ALMOST TWO DECADES THAT HAVE PASSED SINCE Jim Faro first proposed the then-radical notion of con-

---

Left: *Because she is so tolerant of humans and allows close-up looks at common as well as seldom-seen behaviors, Teddy is the favorite of most visitors.* **Inset:** *Where else on this earth can people mix with dozens of brown bears and have very little effect on their behavior?*

Although the exact age of White Claws is unknown, he was thought to be in his late twenties when this photo was taken. In recent years he has not been seen, and sanctuary employees speculate that he has died of old age.

Ms. Mouse and her cubs watch fishing activity on Mikfik Creek.

trolling human activity within the McNeil River sanctuary, not a single visitor has been harmed by a bear, and no bear has been harmed by a visitor. Considering the often close proximity of the two species, and the number of bears present, the program has been an incredible success.

The sanctuary was created with the original intent of protecting the concentration of bears. It was the one place in the world where a person could go to see such a gathering of bears. The early harm done by unrestricted and unlimited visitation has been reversed.

"There are several ways to measure the success of the program: safety, bear numbers, quality of visitor experience, protection of the sanctuary habitat," Aumiller says. "Some factors are hard to measure. Certainly we have maintained the concentration of bears. You come over that little rise there and—Boom!—all of a sudden in front of you are forty or fifty bears all at once. It is an indescribable feeling.

"But there's more. In my mind, the tolerance shown by the bears is probably of equal importance. This tolerance toward humans has become the cornerstone of the McNeil experience.

"Elsewhere bears are treated according to the stereotype of an animal who is a menace to people. Our program demonstrates that that view is not quite right. Bears aren't what we commonly perceive them to be. We have created a safe situation, and bears are willing to accommodate us. They are apparently far more willing to put up with us, than we are with them."

"McNeil wipes away illogical fears," Faro adds. He also points out that the program has been a success because it has been designed to take into account the biological characteristics of the species. "We stay within their biological limitations and don't try to impose our desires on them and attempt to modify their basic behavior."

The future challenge to the sanctuary lies outside its boundaries. In the big picture, human population growth poses a risk to wildlife and natural lands everywhere—McNeil River no exception. In areas of expanding human exploitation, those animals that people perceive to be dangerous, or of no value as a resource worth maintaining for fur or food, are likely the first to be killed off. Human attitudes must change if bears are to survive over their current range. As humans we tend to be afraid of things that we do not understand. Any knowledge gained about wildlife that can be used to paint a clearer picture of an animal's true nature is of incalculable importance. However, if there is no habitat left to support bears, it will not matter what sort of human attitudes prevail. To have bears, we must have large chunks of undeveloped land.

"Alaska in my mind is no different than anywhere else; we're just in a different stage of evolution," Aumiller says. "Growth is real, no matter the rate at which it occurs. Given enough time, the effects of growth reach some level that has irreversible impact. Those areas that are earmarked for certain use, like McNeil, have the highest potential to remain until the last. But eventually they could go. They can't exist as islands."

Faro points out, "The critical factor for McNeil is what happens to the private and state lands to the north and west. What happens to these holdings will make or break McNeil. We don't encompass enough home ranges to fully protect bears without cooperative effort. I'm concerned about the state Department of Natural Resources's plans for surrounding lands. Mining roads, fishing lodges, and land disposals would lead to the loss of bears and bear habitat."

Land-use patterns and resource extraction eventually wiped out the grizzly over much of the western United States and central Canada. Alaska is viewed by many as a giant treasure house of resources just waiting to be exploited. Such thinking bodes ill for species such as brown bears that require large tracts of undisturbed land.

"There is a critical message to get across to Alaskans," Dick Sellers says. "We must realize that we face in Alaska the same forces that killed off the bears in the lower forty-eight. And the way to coexist is to modify human behavior. If we can get the message across and get people to cooperate, then there's room here for bears for a long time to come."

In 1991, the Cook Inlet Aquaculture Association, an organization of commercial fishermen, constructed a $2.7-million fish ladder at the mouth of Paint River, Charles McNeil's river of dreams. Instead of a bonanza in mineral ore, fishermen hope to reap huge catches when this fisheries development project begins producing large runs of salmon. Prior to this "fisheries enhancement" project, the Paint River was perhaps the largest watershed in Cook Inlet without salmon.

Plans to create this artificial run sparked intense public controversy in late 1990 and through much of 1991. At issue is the elaborate fish ladder which will enable salmon to swim around a thirty-five-foot waterfall near the mouth of the river. This fishpass allows salmon access to extensive spawning grounds. Law suits to stop it proved unsuccessful, and the ladder was built in 1991 under the terms of a U.S. Corps of Engineers permit. With this ladder, commercial fishing ventures expect the river to provide increased harvests in lower Cook Inlet where dismal catches have been recorded in the late 1980s and early 90s.

At first glance, it appears that a salmon run on Paint River would perhaps benefit bears by offering an additional food source. Perhaps additional viewing areas would develop. But some people believe that the run could endanger the bears by drawing them out of the sanctuary and into inevitable conflicts with people using adjacent lands. The bears attracted away from McNeil would be subject to sport hunting. Sport fishermen and -women attracted to the area could lead to increasing bad encounters between people and bears and alter the way McNeil bears behave around people. Private hunting and fishing lodges and cabins could be built, and if bears begin to get fish from people or to obtain human food and garbage—or are shot and wounded—safety within the adjacent existing sanctuary could be compromised.

Once commercial fishing of the new runs begins, the native salmon bound for McNeil, Mikfik, and other Kamishak Bay rivers could be caught, critics also charge. Much of the fishing for those stocks already takes place in the vicinity of Paint River. For many people the risks outweighed any potential gains. "There are certain things so precious they should not be put in jeopardy. McNeil River is one of them," emphasizes visitor Steve Tarola.

Since the Alaska Department of Fish and Game manages both salmon and bears, this state agency needs to address concerns on both sides of the issue. Its representatives have stated publicly that a management plan could be developed that would eliminate or minimize most of the conflicts. Critics doubted that a highly politicized agency could accomplish its stated goal of protecting both bears and fishing interests.

One major concern is fear that a large salmon run in the Paint River would draw bears away from McNeil Falls.

"At first, subadult bears dispersing from McNeil, if they encountered rich fishing sites on Paint River, would likely key in on them," Sellers speculates, "and once established there, those bears may not return to the falls. They would be occupying an open-habitat niche. Over a period of time, separate populations would form, one 'loyal' to each drainage. There likely would also be an interchanging population, a group that uses both drainages. I doubt if bears would abandon McNeil en masse. However, it would be critical to manage both drainages with as much consistency as possible."

Critics of the project are unconvinced by such arguments. "It'll be like the Klondike Gold Rush of bears once Paint River is stocked with salmon," says Jack Hession, a Sierra Club representative.

"No one knows what will happen," points out Tony Dawson, a widely published wildlife photographer and leading opponent of the fish ladder. "Why risk this treasure based on speculation?"

Many biologists also voice serious concerns about the project. They speculate that human-bear conflicts will arise, but few seem to think that bears will abandon McNeil River.

"My guess on the Paint River situation," Faro says, "is that when McNeil cubs go off on their own, they may identify with Paint River and not come back. Adult bears won't be that affected. Some of the young bears may switch to Paint River, and there will be some loss that way. I don't see a problem with limited hunting, but I do with any type of development there. The state offering land there for lodges and homesites would be a disaster."

Unrelated to the controversy concerning Paint River are renewed concerns about mineral development. Mining of Charles McNeil's old Paint River claims, the rights to which are now held by a large international mining corporation, could lead to habitat loss, which kills bears and other animals and plants indirectly, as well as to direct killing.

Responding to concerns, the Alaska state legislature in 1991 expanded the original 85,000-acre McNeil River State Wildlife Sanctuary to include the lands at the mouth of Paint River and a small tract to the south. A total of 30,600 acres were added to the sanctuary. A large portion of the surrounding land in the north—about 132,500 acres—was designated the McNeil River State Game

Remote and storm-tossed Kamishak country is often lovely, yet inhospitable to people—a perfect place for bears.

A young bear scans McNeil Cove from a safe vantage point at sunset.

The youngest and least dominant bears are often relegated to fishing sites well away from McNeil River Falls, those along Mikfik Creek. This young bear searches for dead salmon.

Above: *This young bear climbs onto a piece of driftwood to give it the "taste test"—more a form of play than an actual search for food.* **Right:** *Named because of her forsaken adolescent demeanor, Waif grew into a confident adult.*

McNeil River State Game Sanctuary is accessible only by boat or plane. The vast majority of visitors arrive by air. Bill deCreeft has been flying his Dehavilland Otter from Homer to the sanctuary for over two decades.

Refuge. According to the act, the purposes of the refuge are to provide for the permanent protection of brown bears, other wildlife including fish, and their habitats; to manage human use and activities to ensure their compatibility with the protection of the bears; and to provide opportunities for human use that is compatible with the protection of bears. Thus far, sport hunting, fishing, and mineral development are allowed in the refuge.

The act also states that the refuge management plan must address all uses, including "viewing of bears and other uses of fish and wildlife, fishing and fish enhancement, mineral resource development, and traditional, cultural, and historical uses."

Critics charge that the expansion is a start but does not go far enough. They see the proposed artificial salmon run as a continuing threat, and they voice concerns that increased bear hunting in the area now included in the refuge poses a serious threat to bears and humans within the adjoining sanctuary. They are pushing for a hunting closure in the new refuge. The Alaska Board of Game

met in the spring of 1991 but did not approve the closure. Instead, the board endorsed a hunting cap of three bears killed per year in the new refuge and Amakdedori drainage to the north. The board's plan restricts the average annual kill in the 250-square-mile area north of the sanctuary to the historic average annual kill. It also requires the Alaska Department of Fish and Game to create a management plan for the area. Some outdoor groups are pleased that traditional "sport hunting opportunities had been protected," but critics think otherwise.

"Alaska has a wealth of wildlife," writes BBC cinematographer Mike Potts. "Keep it! Development of Paint River could be a big mistake. In theory more fish should be better for man and bears, but it also could lead to a host of problems. I have visited many parts of the world and McNeil River is a very special place indeed. Give the bears a chance."

"It is my personal view that bears using the McNeil River sanctuary are far more valuable to viewers than to hunters," Larry Aumiller says when pressed for his can-

Just as its mother has had long and benign years of encounters with humans, this young cub is just beginning its own journey in trust-building.

did view. "In the larger picture, I feel that all uses of bears are good. The more people who support bears and bear habitat, the better it will be for the long-term survival of bears. Hunters generally support habitat protection. But at McNeil, and in the surrounding area, my personal feeling is that the highest and best use of these bears is for many people to enjoy them throughout the course of each bear's life, rather than for one hunter to have a good experience. We have an enormous amount of time invested in these bears so that they are comfortable around people. It's an investment that should be protected. There are also ethical and safety reasons not to kill, or attempt to kill, bears that people spend time with. Protection for sanctuary bears is in my view so overwhelmingly the right thing to do, that I don't even consider it a debatable position. In time these bears will be protected."

Colleen Matt adds that McNeil bears benefit a vast number of people beyond just those who get to visit the sanctuary. "Photographs in magazines, books, and calendars show bears in intimate ways that few humans have ever seen."

Renowned wildlife photographer Michio Hoshino offers a wider view, "McNeil River must be recognized as being of importance not just to the people of Alaska, and not just to the people of the United States, but to citizens of the entire world. It is a special place that needs special treatment."

In a recent report made at the end of the season, Larry Aumiller summed up the summer's experience. His writing lingers on the biologists' amazement at the close interactions between bears and humans, which continue to be so non-threatening.

"It seems that not only are there more bears but more of them are becoming even more tolerant of humans and their activities. There are, of course, still bears using the area that will not tolerate humans and will leave upon sensing humans, but the most tolerant bears seem ever more able to ignore us. Behaviors like breeding, nursing, and sleeping are commonly seen, often at close range. This season Teddy nursed her two spring cubs eight feet from a small group of astonished humans. Although popular and scientific literature might suggest otherwise, we've come to believe that in the absence of food reward, the more habituated a bear is, the safer it is. This is supported by the record: Even with increased numbers of bears, and people, each year we have fewer marginal situations in dealing with bears (bears in camp, bears in the garbage burning area, false charges, encounters with stressed bears.) This year there were NO charges, NO bears in the garbage, and very few bears in camp."

The McNeil experience, humans mixing with bears, is a grandiose experiment that offers hope that humans and bears can coexist. Perhaps lessons can be learned which may influence decisions on bears and land use elsewhere.

As bear biologist Charles Jonkle reflects, "If people can learn to live with bears, there's a good possibility that we can learn to live with other people. In short, to live with ourselves. It's based on the give-and-take that's required to live with bears. With them we have to go through a process wherein we learn to trust them and learn to accept the small amount of risk. Perhaps we can accommodate bears. And develop a philosophy that we can share the earth."

Manny, White's offspring, pauses along the shore of Mikfik Creek with her first two cubs.

INDEX

After a summer of fishing and grazing, the long sleep of winter awaits the bears of McNeil River.

About the Author

TOM WALKER, A TWENTY-FIVE-YEAR RESIDENT OF ALASKA, is a freelance writer and photographer specializing in Alaskan and Canadian wildlife. Author of six other books, including *Alaskan Wildlife*, *Shadows on the Tundra*, *Denali Journal*, and *Building the Alaska Log Home*, Walker has also been published in hundreds of newspapers and magazines including *Field & Stream*, *Outdoor Life*, and *Alaska*. His photos have been seen in publications such as *Sierra*, *Audubon*, and *National Geographic*.

About the Photographer

LARRY AUMILLER HAS BEEN SANCTUARY MANAGER AT McNeil River State Game Sanctuary for the Alaska Department of Fish and Game since 1976. He first became interested in bears after watching an early National Geographic special about the Craighead brothers' bear research in Yellowstone National Park. In 1984 he had the honor of escorting the Craighead family to McNeil River falls. Dubbed "the Dian Fossey of bears," Aumiller plans, much to the consternation of his friends, to be buried in the sanctuary.

Left: *As biologist Charles Jonkle has said, perhaps by learning to live with bears, humans can learn to live with one another.*

READINGS

Readers will uncover a wealth of facts and photographs about the fascinating brown/grizzly bear in the following books:

Bledsoe, Thomas. *Brown Bear Summer*. New York: E.P. Dutton, 1987.

Craighead, Frank C., Jr. *Track of the Grizzly*. San Francisco: Sierra Club Books, 1979.

McNamee, Thomas. *The Grizzly Bear*. New York: Alfred A. Knopf, 1984.

Murie, Adolph. *The Grizzlies of Mt. McKinley*. Washington, D.C.: U.S. Department of Interior National Park Service, 1981.

Murray, John A. (editor), *The Great Bear*. Anchorage/Seattle: Alaska Northwest Books, 1992.

Schneider, Bill. *Where the Grizzly Walks*. Missoula, MT: Mountain Press Publishing Co., 1977.

Schullery, Paul. *The Bears of Yellowstone*. Yellowstone Park, WY: Yellowstone Library and Museum Association, 1980.